# Reading the World
## what young children learn from literature

# Reading the World
## what young children learn from literature

*Sandra Smidt*

**Trentham Books**

Stoke on Trent, UK and Sterling, USA

Trentham Books Limited
Westview House    22883 Quicksilver Drive
734 London Road   Sterling
Oakhill            VA 20166-2012
Stoke on Trent     USA
Staffordshire
England ST4 5NP

First published 2012

**British Library Cataloguing-in-Publication Data**
A catalogue record for this book is available from the British Library

Cover credit: My thanks go to Giordano Martinelli who so generously allowed us to use the original painting by his grandfather Bruno Cordati for the cover of this book

Credit: pages 111/112: We are grateful to David Macaulay and his publishers Houghton Mifflin Harcourt for permission to use these pages to illustrate Macaulay's innovative approach.

ISBN 978-1-85856-505-7

Designed and typeset by Trentham Books Ltd, Chester
Printed and bound in Great Britain by 4edge Limited, Hockley

## Dedication

Hannah was the first of my grandchildren and was born at a time when I was just becoming interested in the development of young children. As the first of a new generation of our family, she was born into an environment full of books and music and talk and she was read to, talked to, sung to, rhymed at, played with, listened to and had every moment of her very early development noted with amazement. And she proved a receptive audience and participant, joining in everything with interest, zeal and emotional engagement. She became an early consumer and maker of narrative and so you find her throughout this book and her presence here needs this explanation to contextualise it. The four grandchildren who followed have also become readers and writers and narrators – each arriving where they are today through their own individual interests, learning styles, experience and culture. Hannah is here solely because she came first and provided a blueprint for what was to follow. So this book is dedicated to them all – Hannah and Chloe, Ben and Jacob and Zac – with my love.

# Contents

Introduction • ix

**Part 1: Setting the scene**

Chapter 1
**The difficult art of narrative • 3**

Chapter 2
**Meaning-Making: a word about semiotics • 15**

**Part 2: Tales told, visualised, read, said,
heard, shared and transformed**

Chapter 3
**'Listen with your nose and eyes':
the power of the oral tradition • 29**

Chapter 4
**Reading the images • 43**

Chapter 5
**The interweaving of pictures with words • 57**

Chapter 6
**The tale visualised in your head • 71**

Chapter 7
**Who's culture is it? • 81**

Chapter 8
**Children's books in translation • 93**

**Part 3: Reading the world**

Chapter 9
**Controversy: the role and significance
of postmodern picturebooks • 109**

Chapter 10
**Making the coin and currency:
the child as narrator • 125**

Chapter 11
**Adopting and subverting the real world
through narrative in role play • 139**

**Building your collection • 153**

**Bibliography • 171**

**Index • 177**

# Introduction

This book arose out of a meeting I attended last year, to celebrate the 25th anniversary of the publication of Beverley Naidoo's book *Journey to Jo'burg*. The title of the meeting was 'Learning through Literature' and it was held at the School of Oriental and African Studies, supported by the British Council and the Canon Collins Trust and hosted by writer and poet Michael Rosen. *Journey to Jo'burg* is a children's book that was banned in South Africa for many years. Present at the meeting were Southern African writers Gillian Slovo, Njabulo Ndebele and Ret-sepile Makamane. It was an entertaining and stimulating meeting and for me it was really significant because it reminded me of what it was like in the days before the national curriculum and the literacy hour, the days when reading to children was an essential and important part of every nursery and school day. Through the poems and rhymes and stories and tales we read and told we were able to stimulate the imagination of the children and help them to become critical and creative thinkers.

At the meeting Michael Rosen asked the panel to talk about their own experiences of literature in their early years. It was here the Njabulo and Ret-sepile reminded the audience that not all literature is written. Their own childhood experiences involved a great deal of listening to the traditional tales and rhymes and chants of their communities and cultures. And both Gillian and Michael, growing up in politically conscious and 'progressive' Jewish families talked about books that were not approved of – and hence became doubly desirable. Gillian most wanted to read the books of Enid Blyton and Michael most wanted to read comics. These were disapproved of by their parents on the grounds of being politically and/or socially unacceptable in terms of the attitudes displayed.

I have been thinking about the importance of narrative in the lives of young learners for a long time now, particularly through my interest in the work of

Vygotsky and Bruner. Both believed that children are active constructors of meaning and that narrative is a fundamental part of this meaning-making. Through my own experience both as a reader and as an educator I know just how much can be learned from exploring and experiencing the narratives of others. So that was my starting point.

This book is *not* about about using literature to teach children to read. Nor is it about teaching children to write. I will not be talking about phonics or points of grammar. Rather, I hope the book will persuade you – the reader – to read to the children, tell them stories, invite them to tell you stories and in this way draw them into the wonders of narrative. I hope it will help you ensure that the literature you introduce reflects the languages and experiences of the children in your group and that you will find ways of welcoming books and stories in other languages into your setting and asking older children or parents and grandparents to read or tell stories to the children. You can also invite in professional storytellers who use a range of devices to draw everyone into the story being told.

The aim of this book then is to encourage all those working with children – even very young children – to spend time thinking about what rhymes and tales and chants and songs and stories to read to them and tell them. You will learn about some of the specific features of books and stories that are most likely to appeal to children and allow them to make links with their own lives. You may use this as a way of choosing what to read and tell. You might invite the children to choose and perhaps to bring into the setting stories they particularly like. Your aim is to allow them to learn about the real world and the people in it as well as encounter other imagined, invented and possible worlds. This will help them develop and refine their own abilities as narrators so they are able to construct their own stories using some of the devices found in books and stories. These include the very language of books: the use of repetition, rhythm and rhyme; of unusual words and metaphor and simile. These devices offer children a chance of seeing how authors create characters, sequence events, introduce trouble and suspense and drama – all of which invite children to be drawn into the narrative and to find aspects of themselves or their families and friends in the characters and events they encounter.

This book is traditional in structure in the sense of being divided into parts and chapters. Each chapter starts with a quotation, many from the wonderful poems collected to celebrate mothers and called *love to mama* (Mora, ed, 2001) and some from other books.

1. Part 1 is called *Setting the scene* and is made up of two chapters. The first looks at the difficult art of narrative and the second looks at children making meaning and at semiotics. These two chapters provide some theoretical foundation for what follows.

2. Part 2 is called *Tales told, visualised, read, said, heard, shared and transformed*. Here you will find chapters on the oral tradition, on wordless picturebooks, where I use the convention of referring to picturebooks – rather than 'picture books' as Nikolajeva and Scott do – on picturebooks, on 'chapter' books, on popular culture and on translation. Each of these chapters has a section on: the themes explored within the particular genre being discussed, the work the children have to do to make meaning, and what you, the adult, can do in order to help children make meaning. It is in this last section that I talk about building a pedagogy around narrative and literature.

3. Part 3 is called *Reading the world* and here there are chapters on controversy in literature, on children as narrators and on what children can do to both adopt and subvert the world through role play.

4. At the end of the book is section called *Building Your Collection* which consists of titles of all the children's books referred to in the text. Some are annotated. There are classic children's books together with newer books. It is a largely personal selection and you should certainly not be bound or limited by it. The books are included because I had so much pleasure reading and researching them that I wanted to share my passion for books with you.

There are many people to thank in connection with this book.

(a) Firstly my thanks go to my friend Hazel Abel who read the book in draft for me, as she has done with many of my books. I very much value her opinion.

(b) My thanks also go to Giordano Martinelli who so generously allowed us to use the original painting by his grandfather Bruno Cordati for the cover of this book.

(c) Thanks are due also to colleagues at Canon Collins Trust and the British Council whose conference on the importance of literature to learning was the inspiration for the book and to Gillian Klein whose own values and belief in the book enabled her to risk publishing it.

(d) And to all those who, wittingly or not, contributed their own narratives or shared their views and preferences with me.

# Part 1
# Setting the scene

# 1

## The difficult art of narrative

Once there was a Super Mighty Mouse.
Once there was Superman.
Superguy too.
Then Jack came.
(Paley, 1988:px)

The main purpose of this book is to remind all those involved in the lives of young children of the importance to their learning and development of 'literature'. Certain key terms need to be defined for the purposes of this book and some issues addressed. In this opening chapter I define what I mean by literature and also childhood; think carefully about the role of narrative and storying as ways of making sense of the world and consider the significance of books and other things as cultural tools. This takes me into the realms of what constitutes high culture and what popular culture. But I want to start with a story – the true story of 5 year old Hannah who, when invited by her reception class teacher to choose a nursery rhyme to sing and illustrate, chose 'The Lobster Quadrille' from *Alice in Wonderland*. You may remember that it starts like this:

'Will you walk a little faster?'
Said a whiting to a snail,
'There's a porpoise close behind us,
And he's treading on my tail.
See how eagerly the lobsters
And the turtles all advance!
They are waiting on the shingle -
Will you come and join the dance?
Will you, won't you, will you,

Won't you, will you join the dance?
Will you, won't you, will you,
Won't you, won't you join the dance?

Hannah had found this easy to memorise because of the compulsive rhythm and the rhymes and despite the fact that the meaning probably eluded her. When she started illustrating her rhyme she drew a human-like figure and added ears, but then asked for a rubber because there was something wrong with the ears. She explained to her teacher 'I am struggling because I don't really know what a whiting looks like'.

## Defining childhood: whose world is this?

Children's books are written by adults. By implication these adults have a view of their child audience which implies they have a notion of what childhood must be like. But it does not take a great lap of imagination to realise that childhood a century ago was different from childhood today; childhood in rural Africa is different from childhood in urban London; childhood in leafy Surrey is different from childhood in war-torn Aghanistan. And if you take the trouble to analyse the children's books you encounter you will find a growing tendency to move away from reflecting some sort of idealised childhood where the child is seen as good, innocent, powerless, protected by adults, to seeing the child as a player in the world and encountering in it, often through fantasy and possibility, a huge range of experiences, relationships, feelings and ways of being. If you are particularly interested in this Perry Nodelman (2008) has written widely on the subject. The present book argues that it is important to ensure that when you select what stories to read and tell you take account of the kind of childhood reflected to see if it offers opportunities for 'your' children to find aspects to which they can relate.

The creators of picturebooks are largely responsible for moving children's literature to a less narrow view of childhood. The very fact of using images means that writers and illustrators have had to think more carefully about how appropriate the images are to our world. As you read about the books in Part 2, keep this in mind.

## Defining literature: what should be kept in or left out.

Defining literature is difficult partly because narrative in all its forms is so closely tied to cultural contexts, values and norms. Dictionary definitions almost universally link literature to the written word, as these definitions illustrate:

(a) writings in which expression and form, in connection with ideas of permanent and universal interest, are characteristic or essential features, as poetry, novels, history, biography and essays

(b) the entire body of writings of a specific language, period, people and so on

(c) writings dealing with a particular subject, as, for example, the literature of ornithology

(d) any kind of printed materials, as circulars, leaflets or handbills

(Definitions taken from http://dictionary.reference.com/browse/literature (accessed 13/01/11).

Definitions such as these are rooted in the etymology or origins of the word. It moves from the Old French word *litteratura*, meaning alphabet or system of letters or writing, based on the Latin word *litteratus*, which means learned or cultured or erudite, which is based on the Humanistic Latin word *littera*, which means letter or epistle, based on the Greek word *diphthera* meaning skin or leather.

This in itself is not terribly helpful and may seem of little relevance. It certainly raises some questions when we start to think about young children and their strenuous and creative attempts to make sense of their world. If literature refers only to the written word where, for example, do wordless books fit? What about the books that children look at or read at home as opposed to those promoted by their schools? What about the enormous range of stories on film and DVD and other media? Should these come into our definition of literature? Are some books acceptable and others not? Who decides? It seems clear that, in order to move beyond this, we need to ensure that our definition of literature includes the things the children themselves choose. What they choose will almost certainly include digital, visual and other forms of popular current narrative.

## High culture or popular culture

Some time ago I recorded a discussion held between students after attending a programme on reading to and with children. The programme had been designed specifically for teaching assistants. They were asked the question 'Do you think that literature is important in the development of young children?" Here are some of their responses:

Aisha: Literature? You mean Shakespeare and things like that. That's not for small children.

Ben:    I think it is important for children to see other people reading books but I don't think it matters what the books are.

Feliz:    I think older children should read good books – literature – poetry and plays and stuff. But younger children can have picturebooks.

Yvette:   In our reception class the teacher is always going on about the importance of using rhymes to help children sound out words. She never talks about literature.

Babette: In our nursery the teacher reads to the children all the time. She reads them picturebooks and they sing songs and they chant nursery rhymes and sometimes she gets parents in to sing songs or chant rhymes in Bengali or Turkish. I think stories and rhymes are really important in our nursery

Aisha:   That's all lovely but I can't see what it has to do with literature. You are talking about picturebooks and songs and not Jane Austen.

Harriet:  I am not sure about any of this. My own children love films and cartoons and stories on TV or the computer. They watch things like *The Secret Garden* and that's literature, isn't it?

These young people, like many others, clearly think that literature refers to what we might call 'good books' or 'the classics' or high culture. For the purposes of this book, arguing as it does that literature is an essential ingredient in learning and development, we need to broaden the definition so that it relates to the lived experience, needs, interests and concerns of children.

Those now successfully making narratives for children through images and words in books and other forms, and responding to changes in society and technology, draw children into the worlds they create.

Margaret Meek was a teacher, critic and reviewer of children's books. She worked for many years at the University of London Institute of Education and is a much revered figure in the worlds of education, language teaching and learning and children's literature. She was very interested in how children came to be literate in the sense of not only being able to read but wanting to read, understanding the wonders of books and story. For her

> Literature is not old books, not a list of specially chosen great books which represent an unchanging heritage, conferring on the reader the distinction of showing taste and discrimination. There is no way of saying that a text is literature by inspecting its sentences or its formal arrangement. (Meek, 1991:181)

She went on to say that what counts as literature will evolve and develop and change as technologies develop. Accepting this we now have to add to our definition the written literature produced as part of popular culture, as well as the oral literature of stories and rhymes and songs and the visual literature of comics and graphic forms.

What is meant by the term 'high culture' when applied to literature is the sense that a book can only be called literature when it has been determined as being amongst 'the best' that has been produced in a given age. This is a shifting term in that what is regarded as 'best' depends to some extent on who is making the judgement and when. To illustrate this let us take opera, which is often regarded as being part of high culture. Yet in Mozart's day his opera, *The Magic Flute*, written especially to raise funds he urgently needed for basic survival, and was perceived as being part of popular culture. The same is true of much that is labelled literature.

There are the books and other forms of narrative that are considered 'good for children' and there are the books ands rhymes and tales and songs that children choose to read or listen to and which are generally often regarded as being part of popular culture.

Terry Eagleton is one of our most influential living literary critics. In *Literary Theory: an Introduction* he discussed the difficulties of defining literature and said that if literature is defined as 'good' writing, anything can be literature and anything can stop being literature. For him, the term is highly subjective. The implication is that practitioners can welcome into their classrooms and settings whatever interests the children and allows them into the worlds of narrative, written and other. Those working with young children are in the privileged position of being able to push the boundaries for children by offering them a taste of what they might not yet have encountered and in this way introduce them to some of the great and good books and stories whose continued existence is testament to their quality.

## Examining narrative

Essentially in this book we look at the role of narrative in the lives of young children. Narrative – or the making of stories – is how we structure and come to make sense of our own experiences and the experiences of others. Seminal work on narrative was done by Jerome Bruner and he said:

> ...we know that narrative in all its forms is a dialectic between what was expected and what came to pass. For there to be a story something unforeseen must happen. Story is enormously sensitive to whatever challenges our con-

ception of the canonical. It is an instrument not so much for solving problems as for finding them. The plight depicted marks a story's type as much as the resolution. We more often tell stories to forewarn than to instruct. And because of this stories are a culture's coin and currency'. (Bruner, 2002:15)

Bruner is saying that narrative is essentially rule-bound and has to be so that it can be understood; that it sets up a dialogue between the teller and the reader/viewer/listener and that it includes the unexpected for the story to be able to unfold. It also raises questions in the minds of the reader/listener/viewer. There is research evidence in the work of Judy Dunn, Colwyn Trevarthen and others that very young children reveal an ability to understand not only the thoughts but also the feelings of others. This becomes apparent when some of the things very young children say or do are analysed. When 3 year old Hamid noticed the new child in the class crying, he went up to the teacher and announced solemnly, 'He sad.' For this young child to be able to say this he must have not only understood the link between crying and sorrow but also recognised it in another person. This is known as *intersubjectivity* and is essential to being able to live together with others. The existence of a shared culture built of common norms and expectations, often embedded in our cultural stories, is what allows this to happen. This is why Bruner says story is the 'coin and currency' of culture.

A story or narrative requires characters who have their own minds and thoughts and ideas: these characters share expectations of the world of the story. Dystopian novels, like *Animal Farm* or *The Year of the Flood* introduce characters who conform to or rebel against the created norms and expectations, the rules or the customs created by the story maker. A story also requires a narrator or a teller and a listener or a reader. In Martin Waddell's *Owl Babies* three little owls sit on a branch waiting for their mother to come back with their food. They expect their mother to return but fear that she may not. They share both expectations and feelings, and children looking at the book are pulled into sharing these expectations and feelings. The dialogic nature of the story involves the voice of the narrator and the eyes, ears and mind of the reader/viewer/listener.

Children enter the world of narrative very young. Through everyday experience they develop expectations of what their world will be like and often show particular interest in the unexpected or the strange.This is evident in their early play. When, for example, they are involved in games of peekaboo – those often wordless dramas where something unexpected happens – they are delighted. They want the ritual repeated again and again. They reveal what Bruner calls 'narrative precocity' (Bruner, 2002:32), meaning an ability, heard and recorded by him and his colleague Joan Lucariello, in the bedtime soliloquies of an American child called Emmy. In her musings on the events of her day Emmy often reflected on something unexpected or surprising that had happened. But not only did she reflect on how she had dealt with the events but she also predicted what she might do in a similar situation in the future. For Bruner this was evidence of the child knowing what a story needs for its telling. At the very least a story needs a beginning, some happenings, including suspense or surprise, and an ending.

The essence of being a narrator is being able to represent and re-represent things in story form. You were introduced to 5 year old Hannah at the beginning of this chapter. Here she is again, even younger this time, and becoming a narrator.

> On the long drive from Johannesburg to Cape Town a petrol station offered a free set of brightly coloured plastic dinosaur moulds. When they arrived in Cape Town it was raining so they could not go out and Hannah's set only got played with after she had watched the film of *The Secret Garden* on television. This complex story about an orphaned girl and her interactions with a group of people and animals in a strange and gloomy Yorkshire setting offered Hannah little familiar to relate to. her own experience was of living in multicultural, multi-lingual sunny South Africa. Yet she did have her vast experience of books read and told which gave her experiences of narrative, of a rich fantasy world and of characters with likes and dislikes, fears and loves and, very often, with powers. For her, the robin who leads the children to the secret garden was 'believable' in a made-up world. As she watched the film alongside adults she became involved in the story and was guided through it by her questions and the responses of the adults.

> When the dinosaurs were taken to the beach next day Hannah proceeded to use them to represent the characters in *The Secret Garden* as she reconstructed and acted the story as she remembered it. She chose which characters and objects should be represented and these included the heroine of the story, Mary; the boy, Dickon, who befriends her; his horse and his sister; her invalid cousin Colin; the precious skipping rope she was given and the robin that led her into the secret garden.Colin's uncle, whose transformation at the end of the book makes this into a story with a happy ending, was ignored, as was the nasty housekeeper.

> Using the sand on the beach and the plastic characters, Hannah set up scenes and played them out, moving the characters around to carry out the actions she

intended for them. She has become the story maker, the narrator. This play extended over several days and it was interesting that each character in the story
was always represented by the same plastic dinosaur. The themes she explored related primarily to the robin leading Mary and Dickon into the secret
garden, Colin being sick but eventually feeling well enough to join them outside,
and the planting of seeds to make the garden bloom. (Based on Smidt, 2001:
26)

Narrative, then, is at the heart of making sense of the world and becoming
part of that world. As children hear more and more narratives in the form of
stories read and told, poems read and told, rhymes and jingles chanted, songs
sung, films watched and so on, they begin to make links between their experiences and those of others and begin to create their own narratives.

## About culture and cultural tools

Bruner talked of narrative or story being the coin and currency of *culture*. Culture is a word often used, although not always carefully enough. To understand better we need to consider some of the work of Lev Vygotsky, the great
Russian thinker, working in the early decades of the last century. He was a
theorist who was deeply concerned with situating his argument within the
context of both history and culture and is described as taking a sociocultural
or sociohistorical perspective. By 'cultural' Vygotsky meant the ways in which
societies organise both the many tasks which the growing child encounters
and the tools – some mental and some physical – the child is introduced to to
help her master these tasks. Physical tools like pencils and hoes and hammers
are easy to understand. They are things people have developed so as to make
some essential tasks easier to accomplish. Cultural tools are things that have
developed to facilitate communication within groups. Books are an example
of a cultural tool.

Both the tasks and the tools will differ from culture to culture. A child growing
up in Florence in Italy may have her own cot to sleep in in her own room with
pictures hanging on the wall. A child growing up in Soweto in South Africa
might sleep in a lined box or in the same bed as her parents. The Western
child might explore soft toys and the African child an empty tin. Both children
are coming to make sense of their world through their explorations – through
touching and tasting and looking and listening and feeling and interacting
with others. Both children are growing and developing in a social context and
both have their experiences bathed in language. With his historical hat on,
Vygotsky was concerned with how human beings have mastered and continue to master their environment, and greatly interested in the development

of language, which is a way of communicating, within a culture, the generalised concepts of that culture.

Our European and our African baby will encounter narrative, almost certainly
in different forms. One may well have stories read whilst the other may have
stories told, and the stories themselves will have developed within each of the
cultures. In some societies the development of stories told became the
development of stories recorded and fixed in the books. The stories themselves and the books they may become are both cultural tools: they are ways
in which human beings within a culture are able to communicate their ideas
and thoughts to one another. What is significant about cultural tools is that
they change our thinking. They do so by allowing us to reflect on or remember
things we have experienced. So there is a close link with memory. Think of the
stories you were told as a child or the stories you tell your own children and
how often they relate to what happened to you or to the teller of the tale.

Some examples illustrate how cultural tools themselves shape our thinking
and draw us into our historically accumulated store of meanings and ways of
doing things:

■  Sacha's dad tells him stories from Russia, in Russian, whilst his mum
    sings him English songs and plays lots of predictive games which always
    end with a surprise.

This child is being inducted into the cultural store of the cultures of both his
parents.

■  Xoliswe carries her baby on her back and the baby observes all aspects of
    daily life. Often Xoliswe tells the baby what she is doing, even though the
    baby is only three months old.

Xoliswe's baby is being drawn into the rituals of her mother's culture through
being physically present and being talked to throughout daily routines.

■  At school the older children are sometimes invited to come into the garden
    of the nursery class to play ring games with the younger ones.

The older children, in this case, are inducting younger ones into the playground
games and rituals of that school. (Smidt , 2009:24)

### The language of narrative – written and spoken

Our definition of literature includes things that are not necessarily written,
but we need to be clear that all narratives – all literature – depend on language. We need to define language so that we share an agreed meaning. A

commonsense definition would describe language as the *communication* of ideas, thoughts and feelings through a system of *signs*, where signs can include sounds, gestures, images or written symbols. The system would be *rule-bound* to allow for those sharing a language to be able to communicate. A child involved in a narrative act as story maker, story listener or story reader uses language to make sense of the story.

Here are some case studies of young children making narratives of their own, always related to their own experience – which may be of books, of TV programmes, of shared games, of toys and so on.

- The first is Jamie, a child in a nursery class at a school in East London at which story was used as a unifying mechanism and the vehicle to meet the diverse language and learning needs of the children.

  Jamie is deftly folding paper to make an aeroplane, he tells me his nanny showed him how. 'They have lights. Buzz is ... Buzz is driving ... 321 blast off ... oh no, its wings has come off ... it's died'. (Kelly, 2004:72)

Engaged in an activity involving him making something of his own choice, Jamie constructs a running narrative as he works. The Buzz referred to is Buzz Lightyear, a character from *Toy Story* Jamie is intimately familiar with and very interested in. He uses language and that language reflects the subject matter. It is unlikely that he would count down from three in relation to anything other than blasting off!

- The second child is aged 6 and a half and her name is Sundari. Like Hannah she had fallen in love with nonsense rhymes. Her narrative shows really clearly how she has drawn on *The Quangle-Wangle's Hat* by Edward Lear. She is so attuned to the language of stories that she even has the confidence to invent her own nonsense words.

  Once upon a time there was a tree ... not an ordinary tree ... a tree with eyes and ears and a mouth and a very round nose and this tree had legs and arms not ordinary arms ... but brick arms it was called the quoggly woggly tree and it walked all about with the other quiggly quoggly trees and the quoggly quoggly trees now the quiggly quoggly trees are the girls and the quoggly quoggly trees are the boys. (Fox, 1993:44)

Sunari's use of language is astounding and she is a skilled story teller, using many of the devices she has encountered in her rich linguistic background of story, song, rhyme, book, film and other narratives. I find her concern to assign trees to different gender groups fascinating. Both of the children cited here draw on the experiences they have had of story and poetry, films and other narrative forms.

■  The next child is a 4 year old Gurdeep, a bilingual Punjabi-English speaking child in the reception class. Like the other children in his class he is in the early stages of learning to read and his experience includes narratives from books and from oral stories told in Punjabi. He and his sister share a bedtime story read by their father. The chosen book comes from the local library and it is written either in English or with dual text, but chosen to help the children retain some sense of the culture of India. In school Gurdeep became involved in playing with some puppets based on Where the *Wild Things Are* and then picked up the book and began his own re-telling of the story. This is an edited/abbreviated version.

He went to sleep with no dinner. The bedroom grow ... grewed and grewed ... his mother said Your ... I called you wild Max. He buyed ... he buyed a private boat that came out of ... Out of the water came a big monster and he (blows) did that and Max was scared then they went down. Down he went. He said I'm coming out. They gnashed their terrible ... gnashed their terrible eyes ... Tashed their terrible. Tashed their terrible teeth and ... showed their terrible claws. Then Max said Don't just get off this ground. I'm going to be the king. He danced and he danced ... and danced and had a fight. Then he said goodbye and they said we'll eat you up. (Minns, 1990:60)

In this re-telling of a story Gurdeep used some of the language of the book itself – phrases like 'private boat'. It is unlikely that that phrase would be part of his English language experience or usage. He also recalls phrases like 'gnashed their terrible teeth and in his re-telling we can sense the pace and the rhythms of the original story.

■  Emir is a Turkish child, recently arrived in England. He learned English quickly and proved himself an able learner and joined in with all classroom activities. Most of all he liked to tell stories and his teacher was intrigued that a particular character featured in all the stories he wrote and told. So she asked him about it. 'Who is this *Hodja* you are always talking about?' He looked at her, astonished that she – a teacher – did not know. 'He is our storyteller – he plays tricks on people and is very funny. Also brave and wise.' In response the teacher ordered some of the Hodja stories for her class. (Personal communication)

## The implications of all of this for you, the adult

■ We all make sense of our experience through narrative so it is important to encourage children in doing this by reading to them, telling them stories, looking at books with them, providing books for them, singing songs, introducing rhymes and chants and showing that stories matter.

■ Sometimes parents are anxious to know that children are learning at school and it is up to you to explain to parents and carers why books and stories and narratives in all forms are important for children's learning and development. Not only are they pleasurable but they are also cognitively challenging, helping children to raise and answer questions, to make links with their own experience and to remember things that are important to them.

■ Explicitly recognise and respect the differences encountered in our classrooms and settings in terms of prior experience, home and community languages, styles of interaction, how story is perceived by different groups and so on. So be careful in your choice of what stories to read and tell and show, ensuring that they reflect appropriate views of childhood, address the issues which matter to the children and present high quality content, language and images.

■ Recognise the individuality of children and invite them to bring their own personal interests and concerns into the setting. This implies having a dual responsibility, both to introduce children to the things of particular value in their lives, learning and development, and to show respect for the things that interest and fascinate them – that is what is called popular culture.

# 2

## Meaning-Making:
## a word about semiotics

When our grandmothers
come to visit, they bring us
gifts, *regalitos* as they say
in Spanish, like sweet
caramelo. They bring us
stories from their childhoods in Cuba...
(from *Las abuelitas* by Virgil Suarez)

In this chapter we look at semiotics (signs and symbols) and look briefly at metaphor and its uses, examine differences between the symbolic and the realistic, consider the importance of the imagination and touch on poetry and film.

Semiotics is the study of sign systems.When we think about children's literature we are thinking of a range of different sign systems, beginning with the spoken words which make up our own language. Through experience we use language to make and share meanings with one another. Each word uttered can be represented as a set of alphabetic symbols, which are converted into the sounds of our language, and convey a meaning.

Saussure (1857-1913), who talked a great deal about semiotics, was a linguist who became interested in not only his own language of French, but in language itself. He talked of the linguistic sign as being a two-sided entity which he called a dyad. On one side was the signifier – the thing that makes the sign. In the case of a spoken word the signifier is the voice, specifically the vocal cords. In writing the signifier would be the pen or the computer keyboard or the printing block. Inseparable from this is the signified and this is harder to understand. It is the meaning or, as Saussure would have it, the mental concept. Take a common word like 'cat'. It is made up of three signifiers c/a/t but what is signified is not a real cat but some concept or image or idea of a cat. I might see a small grey cat with green eyes whilst you might think of a sleek Persian cat and the person next to you might think about her allergy to cat hair and the person opposite you might recall the soft sound of purring. Each of us has a mental notion of what we might call 'catness'. For Saussure the inseparability of the signified and the signifier is what allows us to share our thoughts and ideas – the contents of our minds.

This is what happens when we start thinking about story and narrative – the thoughts of the writer or artist, transmitted through the voice or the images or the two together, enter our minds and influence what is already there and allow us to build new images, concepts, thoughts, ideas and feelings. We come to each listening or reading with our unique experience and so the story we hear or make or see or read is interpreted differently by each of us.

Consider how an artist displays or depicts or organises images in a way that allows them to be interpreted by whoever looks at them according to their own experience. The pictures are intended to be 'read' or to allow the viewer to lift the message from the page. But the message is not fixed. It is up to the reader of the image to draw on her own experience and understanding to decide a meaning and create a narrative. In a very similar way written words made up of alphabetic symbols are also capable of being read in order to find meaning. But written language is rule-bound and this limits but does not exclude interpretation. The words on the page remain the same all the time so there is less scope for individual interpretation.

The work of Gunther Kress about semiotics is fascinating. His focus is almost entirely on how children make meaning. Since this book is about what children, primarily young children, can learn from and though literature, we need to try – with Kress's help – to see meaning-making not through the eyes of the adult but through the eyes of the child. This will help us respond to children's meaning-making more appropriately.

## The importance of interest to making meaning

Many schooling systems operate on the assumption that there are bodies of knowledge that need to be passed on from one generation to another. This is what constitutes the curriculum – national, local or individual. The underpinning philosophy of a curriculum may be that of inducting children into the adult world. Childhood is seen not as a phase in its own right – despite many protestations to the contrary – but as preparation for adulthood. Too often we ignore what children already know and – significantly – what they are interested in or passionate about – in order to 'teach' them something new. Later in this book you will find a discussion between two adults about about what to do if a child responds to a book with a seemingly unrelated comment. It would be easy to ignore this but, as a sensitive adult who is interested in what the child's response means, you would try and work out what this might be.

Kress says that *interest* is a significant feature of making meaning. What he means by interest is what the child is paying attention to, fascinated by or interested in. As children make meaning they begin to use signs and the question arises of signs are made in particular ways. Why, for example, do most young children draw the human figure with a very large head and rather long legs? Is this incompetence, a factor of immaturity or is it because this is what an adult looks like from a child's viewpoint? For Kress interest is a composite of our experience: when someone makes a sign they do so in light of their likes and dislikes, their experience, culture, language and identity – their interest. When children start making their own signs – letters, shapes, words, images – we need to look at them in light of what we think the child's experience has been and what her interests are. Similarly we need to attend equally carefully to the interjections or comments children make during the sharing of narrative.

Kress tells us that signs come about as the result of our actions in the context of culture and with the aim of communication. Kress uses the term *motivated signs* for the signs we devise that are closely related to meaning. If, for example, we need a sign to distinguish between male and female toilets we often use symbols depicting someone in a skirt and someone in trousers. This is a straightforward and conventional relationship between meaning and form in cultures where this is the accepted form of dress, as in the Western world.

But what would we do if we wanted to make symbols to indicate power or strength? What would you invent? Here are examples of what groups in different places and at different times have used to symbolise power. The lightning bolt was chosen by Greeks and Romans and Native Americans to symbolise power; the dragon was used in Eastern Asia and the arrow in ancient Greece. Some children at an inner London school chose keys or money to represent power. 'Keys let you in' said one, and 'money buys you anything' said another.

The person making the sign begins to think not only about how the sign might relate to the shape or purpose of the concept but also how it will be interpreted or understood by the audience.Signs, then, have a double social motivation: what they mean to the sign maker and what they mean to the interpreter. This is particularly important for those making books for young children, who have to think about what the images and words will mean for the child and how they will enable the child to make meaning. The book maker must have in mind some notion of the audience or the implied reader.

In the children's book *Lima's Read Hot Chilli*, the author David Mills tells the story of how a little girl returns hungry after school, looks for something to eat in her kitchen and, despite her mother's warning not to eat the red hot chilli, she cannot resist. To soothe the burning in her mouth she drinks water, eats ice cream and jelly and mango and finally swallows a jug of cool milk. A simple repetitive story, with lifelike illustrations by Derek Brazell. The author was a teacher in inner London and in that role obviously encountered young children from different cultural backgrounds, who had different experience and spoke English and other languages. In his making of the story Mills probably had in mind readers like the children he had worked with and was able to impute things to them – familiarity with things like ice cream, jelly, milk, tinned spaghetti and sticky sweets for some and for others experience of foods like mango and samoosas and coconut. The motivated signs are the words and pictures. How children then interpret the story will vary according to their experience but they will all be able to make meaning of the whole story – the girl ate something that burned her mouth and then tried to cool it down. Each story you tell or read, each book you share, will be interpreted according to the experience and the culture of the child and if you, the story-teller/sharer and the author and illustrator are skilled enough, no one will be denied access to the overall meaning.

We all live in a world full of signs made by the sign-makers from our culture and others over long periods of time. You may sometimes feel you are not fully part of the same culture as everybody else because you don't have the same first language or the same cultural tools or the same access to a shared past. I know that as someone born and educated in another country there are many references here that bypass me, even though I have lived in England for more than half my life.

Recently I went to see a performance of Gilbert and Sullivan's *The Mikado* – a light opera I was only vaguely aware of and not much valued by my native culture. And although I was able to laugh at the bits that had been updated to reflect modern life, much of it left me feeling slightly puzzled. whilst all around people were beaming with pleasure and recognition. I felt 'othered' –

not admitted to the inner circle of the knowing but relegated to the margins or periphery. This is an experience many children encounter in their years of education and we need to be aware of it. You can do much to draw children from other cultures into a mainstream activity like listening to stories, and you can help them in making meaning.

Everyday wisdom would suggest that we become meaning-makers and narrators through imitation or copying the models around us. Kress argues – and I agree with him – that no child ever copies. What we all do is *transform* what is around us. Kress uses this example to explain. A 3 year old child walking up a steep hill with his family described the hill as being 'heavy.' According to Kress's transformative view of meaning-making the child, not having the customary word in his vocabulary, compared climbing the hill to other physically difficult things he had tried to do – perhaps carrying something heavy – and used that word to describe his feelings. In another example. Sammy, aged about 4, wanting to say something important to her mother, said 'I want to make a proclamation'. Perhaps Sammy had heard a story in which the word proclamation had been used and she adopted it to describe she wanted to do. The children had added words to their vocabularies and imbued the words with new meanings. Heavy for one child now implied not only weighing a lot but difficult: a proclamation for the other implied something that other people do but that I can do too. Both children have transformed their own language. What matters here is that each child has used an incorrect word but in a sense that does not really alter the meaning. You recognise that the word 'heavy' was used to describe not the hill but the effort required to climb it: effort is always required in dealing with heavy things. Sammy did not ask for a proclamation for supper or to go on a proclamation: she used it to describe an intended action.

Seeing meaning-making as being transformative, as Kress does, allows us to explain how we each make our own route into language as we do into all other cultural systems. We might all arrive at standard English (or whatever its 21st century equivalent is), but we will get there by different, personal paths. Children making sense of the world and keen to represent their ideas and thoughts and feelings they can share them with others, do so in different ways, using a variety of materials and means. Children use things they find to represent other things. They may use bits of wire and bottle tops and other found materials to make toys, often with moving parts. They may draw with their fingers on misted surfaces, with twigs in the wet sand on the beach, with chalk on the pavement. They may use string and cardboard and glue and scraps of fabric to make cars and parachutes and human figures and boats.

Children are making their own signs, often using what is to hand and what they use sometimes suggests other possibilities. Paper can be cut and folded, painted, written on, cut out, stuck to and so on.

Thus children act *multimodally* in the things they use and the objects they make and in the use of their bodies. Some aspect of their perception of a person or a place or an object features in what they make and for them this is enough to turn what they have made into that object. Kress tells the story story of a 4 year old who said 'My Gawd, I made it like Australia' when she saw something in what she made which reminded her of what she knew about Australia (Kress, 1997:87). What she made is a *metaphor* for Australia.

Children behave multimodally in their sign-making and books made for children can also be multimodal. Nikolajeva and Scott (2006) talk of mimetic or literal and non-mimetic or symbolic representation. This is academic terminology to describe the particular features of picturebooks where the dynamic relationships between word and picture can carry contradictions between the mimetic (that is close to reality and truth) and non-mimetic (which is open to interpretation) representation.

Maurice Sendak's *Where the Wild Things Are* explores Max's feelings after he has had a conflict with his mother and is sent to bed. The book starts by being close to reality (or mimetic) where Max is alone in his room which is shown in cold colours, representing his feelings about his mother's response to his bad behaviour. Then Max imagines a boat waiting for him, with his name on it and he sails away with nothing in the text or pictures to remind him of home. He converts his chilly room to a warmer landscape so that vines descend from the ceiling and the walls become 'the world all around'. When Max encounters the wild things the pictures take over the narrative and move from the reality of his bedroom to the metaphoric landscape of his dream. So the narrative flows from mimetic to symbolic, sometimes in the text and sometimes in the pictures.

*Imagination* plays an enormous role in the making of signs. The maker of the sign does not have to conform to any boundaries but can follow his or her imaginative processes to produce signs never seen before. We see this in the work of modern book makers like Shaun Tan. In his picturebook *The Red Tree*, which is essentially about depression or sorrow, the images are surreal – strange and haunted and dream-like. The book cover shows a red-headed child figure floating in what looks like a paper boat on a misty surface. The same figure appears on the first wordless page standing on a stool in a field, talking through a loud hailer – her words being symbolised by a torrent of letters of the English language falling from it. Tan started as an artist working on science fiction and horror stories in a small-press magazine when he was still a teenager and has now become known for his political and historical dream-like picturebooks.

Imagination is clearly at work here in the creation of the images and each image is a metaphor for something. It is up to the reader or beholder to decipher the metaphor. One page carries the text 'wonderful things are passing you by' and the full-page image is a window reflected in which are colours and shapes of clouds and flying things (Are they birds or leaves or paper or aeroplanes or something-never-before-seen?). The red-haired child stands looking out of the window at the reader or beholder and at the bottom of the window frame is a lock on which is written the word REGRET. This is not a book to be used with young children *en masse*, but it may be of interest to a more sophisticated child going through some crisis. I showed it to 8 year old Umut who had come to this country as a refugee. He spent a long long time looking at the pictures, sometimes chuckling at things like the giant open-mouthed fish in the streets with people walking past oblivious to them. Then he paid great attention to the picture which shows the red-haired child dressed as a witch on a page full of everyday things converted into other things – a birdcage which is itself a bird, a black cat with a halo, a tiny samovar which looks like a baby dinosaur and so on. All he said at the end was 'Is good' and then he looked at it again and again.

Kress reminds us that it is easier for visual images to be open-ended than it is for language, which depends on the use of units like words and sentences. But poets, through their imaginative use of words and sentences, are able to draw readers or listeners into the images they create through words.

*Mice* by Rose Fyleman

I think mice
Are rather nice.
Their tails are long,
Their faces small,
They haven't any
Chins at all,
Their ears are pink,
Their teeth are white,
They run about
The house at night.
They nibble things

They shouldn't touch
And no one seems
To like them much.
But I think mice
Are nice.

Something about the rhythm and pace makes poems and rhymes memorable and allows children to build their own images from the words. Most playful are the nonsense rhymes of writers like Spike Milligan, Edward Lear, Hilaire Belloc and Mike Rosen. Many invent words which can somehow, within the context of the poem, be understood. In *The Owl and the Pussy-Cat* by Edward Lear an owl and pussy cat go to sea in a pea-green boat, taking with them essential supplies (honey, money, and a guitar.) They decide to get married and this is what happens.

They sailed away for a year and a day,
To the land where the bong-tree grows;
And there in a wood a Piggy-wig stood
With a ring at the end of his nose,
His nose
His nose,
With a ring at the end of his nose.

'Dear Pig, are you willing to sell for one shilling
Your ring?' Said the Piggy, 'I will.'
So they took it away, and were married next day
By the turkey who lives on the hill.
They dined on mince and slices of quince,
Which they ate with a runcible spoon;
And hand in hand, on the edge of the sand,
They danced by the light of the moon,
The moon,
The moon,
They danced by the light of the moon.

Kress writes about *affect*, which is synonymous with dispositions or states of mind and says we all have preferences and that this refers as much to narrative as to anything else. Some of us will have a preference for poetry, others for fiction; some will like to read playscripts, others diaries. It is important that we, as educators, offer children a rich diet so they can experience different styles and genre and voice to find what speaks most directly to them.

## The semiotics of film

Our 21st century children spend much time engaging with screens of one kind and another and many of them choose to watch the same cartoon or film over and over again. These children would probably like to hear the same favourite story read over and over but often adults do not have the time to do so. But it is easy to hit a repeat button and some analysis has been done on the effect of such repetition on children's meaning making. Naima Browne (1999) studied this primarily through observing her own child. She concluded that it is through this repeated watching that children come to understand screen semiotics and conventions – the use of flashback to think about time passing, about the past, present and future. On screen and in books the narrative moves forward logically through a sequence, but within that movement events can go backwards and forwards. Two things can happen at the same time. We find parallel stories. So watching screen narrative can help children's meaning making as watchers and listeners and narrators.

Children can rehearse their understanding of what is real and what is pretend and begin to understand, deconstruct, reconstruct and represent. They can begin to define genres. 'Oh this is just an advert, not the real film' or 'I love these cartoons' or My best films are Pixar movies' or 'I don't watch news'. My friend Hilary told me of 4 year old Elliot who, while watching an item about Dr Who on a news programme on television, flinched when the Daleks were shown. He said he didn't like them and she tried to reassure him by telling him that they were not real. He thought about this for a while and then asked 'But if they are not real why are they on the news?'

It sounds straightforward but this very young child has come to understand that what is seen on television is sometimes about real things and sometimes not and to know that what is seen on the news should be about reality and truth.

In film the dream is often used as the device where magic happens. Think about Dorothy arriving in Oz or Alice going down the rabbit-hole or James and his Giant Peach. When asked if Peter Pan might be a dream, Hannah thought long and hard before answering 'No, it can't be because they would all have had to be dreaming the same thing' (Smidt, 2001:30).

Some theorists argue that the semiotics of film is very different from that of books because that of film involves five different but linked tracks – image, dialogue, noise, music and written materials. The language of books is often said to be single words, but we know that the semiotics of children's books include pictures, words, written sound effects and sometimes songs or dialogue. When the books are read aloud the songs and sound effects and dialogue can all be heard. The only real difference is that in films the images move and in books they don't, although movement is often implied.

## The child's work

The Australian artist/author Shaun Tan has thought a great deal about picture-books for children and if it is enough to expect them to appeal only to young children. He draws our attention to the fact that we all like playing – adults, teenagers and children – and we all like narrative. In playing and making stories we like to look at things from different or unusual angles, seek to find something new in the ordinary and bring our imagination and questioning to analysing everyday experience. We ask 'Why are things like this? How might they be different? What do I feel and why do I feel like this? He thinks that books – all books – should find ways of getting children to question their world. In his book *The Red Tree* he started out by playing with colours and patterns and imagery but then found his paintings becoming darker and more dramatic. He says that what he celebrates about the book is that it is free of the usual constraints of sequence and time. Each page is open to individual interpretation. Primarily what the child has to do is to use the language of signs and symbols to make meaning. This means that they have to work out what the meaning is in the sounds that reach their ears, the black marks on the page and the images. This suggests that the work of the child is to start questioning aspects of her own life and reality.

## Building a culture and pedagogy based on narrative

■ Make sure you know as much as possible about what children already know, what their experience has been and what they are interested in. That is fundamental to all early education – indeed to all education.

■ Examine the books you propose using to see if you think children will find things to identify with and will be able to draw on their previous ex-perience. Don't use this to limit what you choose but take care to draw in children who may not be able to make personal links with the narrative being told, read or looked at.

■ Talk to the children about aspects of semiotics. For example how, in a particular text, some words are written in bold fonts and others not. Or about what having a series of dots like this ... across the page suggests. Draw their attention to the direction of both print and action. Make it possible for children to talk about what they find in the pictures.

- Engage children in more complex books, more elaborate language, more detailed images so they encounter new concepts and ideas.

- Look to see how children in their narratives transform rather than copy as they make meaning.

- Where possible offer children different versions or formats for narratives – things like different tellings of tales, using DVDs, taking children to the theatre and so on.

- When you share books with children think about how these can extend their abilities to think and to be imaginative and creative

- Read poems to the children

- Pay attention to children's meaning making, mark making and interjections.

- Take note of children's preferences

- Offer children a rich diet of songs, stories, rhymes and poems.

# Part 2
# Tales told, visualised, read, said, heard, shared and transformed

# 3

## 'Listen with your nose and eyes': the power of the oral tradition

We are the only species to use speech as our primary way of communicating. We talk and listen so automatically that we rarely stop to think about how the sounds that issue from our mouths or come to our ears are the ways in which we learn how the world works and which allow us to build a shared understanding. To accompany talk we use other communicative means – raising an eyebrow, changing intonation, shrugging, smiling, frowning, gasping and so on. We structure our experience into narratives which are told or written and then heard or read. This chapter is about stories, rhymes, jingles, poems and other narratives told and heard and consider their link with narratives fixed in books or other media.

### Flying cows

Harold Rosen (1984) tells it like no on else. It goes like this:

> 'Listen children', runs the Yiddish folk song, 'listen with your nose and eyes' and listen we did for in the very next line a cow flew over the old gossip granny's roof. What nonsense! Listen with your nose and eyes, cows flying over the rooftop. I should be ashamed to be dealing in such trivial absurdities. And I would be, were it not for the fact that our readiness to listen to and to tell stories is so universal and takes such a variety of forms and is made to serve such a range of functions that flying cows belong with the fundamental processes of the human mind. (p6)

For Rosen the making of stories is really a fundamental process of the mind, the way in which we make sense of our experience. But what does the story maker have to do to make a narrative? Events and people are all around us and it is primarily from these that we construct stories. What we have to do is discover, imagine or invent motives, reasons, causes, feelings, consequences. We have to discover meaning. And then we have to imagine or invent beginnings and endings because in making a story we are being selective in what it will be about and creative in shaping it. Here is a little story cited by Harvey Sachs in his paper *On the analysability of stories by children* (1972).

> The baby cried. The mommy picked it up.

Try to analyse this and then compare your analysis with that of Sachs. His analysis of this speech event is very detailed and far beyond the reach of this book. But we can assume, as he did, that the baby is the child of the mommy. Why do most of us assume that? Is it because we know, from experience, that it is usually the mommy who comforts the baby? Is crying an acceptable thing for a baby to do? How do we know that? Is it because, from experience, we have heard babies cry.? Would the statement still have been a meaningful narrative if it had said:

> The baby opened. The mommy cried?

So in constructing a narrative we have to select episodes of things that interest or concern or worry or frighten or amuse us and then shape them so that the sequence we make allows one thing to flow from another. An act of mind. Another narrative cited in Harold Rosen's papers refers to the story told by 7 year old Brian after he had seen a chick hatch in a bird's nest under the school roof. In reading this there are two things to consider: what Brian had to know to construct this narrative and what interested him.

> When I was look ... leaning against the pole I saw the two ... three baby birds, and they all put their wings out and tried to fly, and when I made a noise, the mother noise, they all put their heads up and flapped their wings and started to fly. And I saw the mother come back. She had a worm in her mouth ... and then she gave it to them ... they only had little wings about this big...' (1984:18)

Brian had obviously seen birds, baby birds and mother birds, and he must have known what sound a mother bird might make so he could try to make that noise himself. He must have known that a word used to describe the movement of wings is 'flapped' and he clearly understood how mother birds feed their young. It was at the point in his story where he started to try and illustrate the span of the bird's wings that the teacher intervened to ask him how big the wings were. She seemed to want the answer in some measurement like inches. The question arises as to whether this is an appropriate or sensitive response to the child's story or whether is it rooted in some conventional thinking about teaching and learning. After all it is simpler to focus on the measurable minutiae of what children know – things that are easy to assess like number, size, colour and so on – than to try and unknot the complexity of thinking that goes into making a narrative. This is a really important point for everyone involved with children. In our interactions with them – particularly around creative things like narrative – we need to be aware of what it is they are trying to do and convey.

## The oral tradition and children's literature

Our culture is no longer an oral culture although there are still some cultures which are – like the Somali culture where it is accepted that orality is the preferred way of representing the culture. Walter Ong (1982) studied oral cultures and believed that storytelling in these cultures takes place in the context of shared experience so that the listeners to the story become part of, or create, a community. Ong argued that the listeners begin to see themselves as equal participants in this community and seldom think about what makes them unique or separate from others. Nodelman takes this thought further and sees children's literature as doing this too. What happens is that children, who are watching or listening in groups, may make individual interpretations and narratives but the sharing of the experience forms them into a protocommunity. Together they feel the push and pull of the question as to whether the story is theirs alone or theirs as a group.

Where there is no print, storytelling is the way in which the values and ideas and history and practices and rituals of a community are passed on from generation to generation. In any telling of a story things can be changed and emphasised, edited out, added to, glossed over, repeated and repeated and memorised. Many stories for young children are retellings of older forms – ancient myths and sagas, based on oral folk tales. Then there are the rhymes, the playing with language, the unchanging forms. Children's literature is rich in the features of oral storytelling – the repetitive nature, the focus on action, motives only guessed at, idealised people and settings, the introduction of fantastic elements in lifelike situations and more. Oral stories are passed on by word of mouth, often changing in the telling, but always relating to the fundamental characteristics of the society and culture in which they are rooted.

The coming of the printing press changed most oral societies into mixed societies. The making of stories continues everywhere, although in less ritualised forms and on a more individual basis than in oral societies. When I was a child growing up in a house full of books there were family stories that were told again and again. Here is one which changed according to the teller and the context.

My oldest uncle, Hymie, loved to gather the children round him and tell stories about his siblings. When the family emigrated from Russia to South Africa Hymie, as the oldest, was charged with the care of his siblings. He both loved and hated the responsibility and he became a great storyteller and subsequently a less great story writer. This is a story we heard over and over again.

> You want to hear the story about Bennie? When he got to see America? What a *shlemiel*! Mind you he was only a little *pisher* then. About this high (he showed with his hands) and with eyes like saucers. So one day we decided to tease him. You all know that he believed anything – everything. You could tell him his nose was blue and he would run to look in the mirror, or that the dog next door had grown to be as tall as a horse. A *meshugannah* kid, really. Anyway, we told him if he wanted to see America he must stick his tongue through the keyhole in the door. And it was winter, and you know about those winters. They were ... FREEZING! Not cold, not very cold, not extremely cold. Freezing. So he gets a little apple barrel, turns it over and stands on it. And what happens? His tongue freezes and gets stuck on the lock. He screams and cries. What a *tummel*! And then your *zeide* comes in and shouts at us and gets some warm water to make the tongue come away from the keyhole. We were in trouble but he always said he could see America. What a *nudnik*!

We loved this story about our favourite uncle and we barely noticed that some of the words were in Yiddish, which we did not speak but could understand in context. The story was always the same but always different. And where there were pauses in the telling we joined in. And when Bennie, the hero or the victim of the story, told his version it was the same, but different. The essence of the story was the same but in his version we felt his pain, his humiliation, his anger at his siblings and his strength (or was he just being obstinate?) in always maintaining that he saw America. 'The streets' he would say 'they weren't paved just with gold. They were paved with gold and jewels. And there were trees with beautiful flowers on them and the sun shone all the time and the ladies wore pretty dresses and had little dogs on leads and Charlie Chaplin was there and there were cakes to eat like this (hands held high in the air) and they were for nothing. No money needed.'

And this stayed the same and different through all its tellings. Sometimes the streets were paved with gold and sometimes it was Esther Williams who was there and sometimes there were fancy cars on the road. Listening to the often repeated stories about our emigrant family gave us a sense of belonging together and a picture of our shared culture of which there was precious little in South Africa. But when I tried, much later, to take some of that culture into my school and told one of the family stories for an Afrikaans oral exam, the story, from Yiddish through English to Afrikaans, became flat and meaningless. Something about writing it down, putting into a fixed format and then re-telling it to an audience who had no way into the meaning, destroyed it.

This personal example illustrates how the telling of a story changes when it becomes fixed in a book. Of course there are advantages. The story can be kept just as it is forever and the fact that the print on the page makes it always the same helps young children learn to read. But there may be something less intimate, less exciting and less engaging about a story read compared to a story told. Think about the power of the voice to convey nuances of emotion and that of the body to visually articulate meaning. And storytelling always takes place in a physical context, perhaps round a fire, on a beach, in your bed, on your grandma's knee, but essentially a physical context redolent of warmth and safety and the familiar. It is clear that print and other 'fixing' devices change societies and change styles of narrating. In telling the story about Bennie my uncle Hymie deliberately included Yiddish. These meant that we, the next generation, had access to some of the language of our past and felt the power and music of it through his voice.

In a fascinating paper on how oral culture is transmitted to the page for Inuit children, Joanne Schwartz talks of how the Inuit writer Kusugak uses English in a style that mimics the flow of the Inuktitut language. He uses some Inuktitut words in his tellings but also writes like this:

> The man-with-no-eyebrows had eyebrows, of course, just as Can't-see could actually see: that was just his name. It was a good name. It had been passed down from generation to generation until it came to him. The first The-man-who-had-no-eyebrows probably had no eyebrows at all or maybe his eyebrows were so faint that people had started to call him 'The-man-with-no-eyebrows'. (Kusugak, 2006:5)

### The legacy of the oral tradition

We are a richly diverse country in terms of the cultures and languages reflected in our schools and settings. Many children come from cultures where the oral tradition is still close to them and their families. The oral tradition is still flourishing in places like Afghanistan, Australia, Canada and Somalia.

We all carry with us aspects of our oral past in the nursery rhymes, folk tales, and the playground rhymes and chants and songs we heard in our homes, on the streets, in the playgrounds. Here are some of the types or genres of oral narrative still evident in our culture.

*Nursery rhymes, finger plays, predictive games* and *playground rhymes* are the little tales and sayings and chants passed on in different ways and probably occurring in all cultures. The Opies (1959), famous for their detailed study of the lore and language of schoolchildren, tell us that there is a difference between nursery lore and school lore. Nursery lore is transmitted to the child in infancy by adults in the community and then down the generations – from adult to child. School lore consists of rhymes and chants made up and transmitted by the children themselves.We hear and see both in our schools and settings. Much is important about both: they are easy to remember, often convey a moral or a message and may well be used to accompany physical actions like skipping. The Opies noted how they often have negative connotations used to taunt other children, be racist and offensive, indicate political affiliations and much more.

*Fairy tales* are tales that can still be found in both oral and written form. They were originally intended for both adults and children and often include characters like goblins, dwarves, giants and only occasionally fairies. They appear to occur in all European cultures and probably in cultures throughout the world. One of the features they share is the happy ending. An analysis of fairy tales and a possible explanation for their continued existence is the fact that they deal with so many controversies through narrative.

Charles Perrault (1628-1703) was the first person known to record them in his book of fairy tales and much later Bruno Bettelheim (1976) analysed them and the role they play in helping children deal with difficult issues. Cruelty, hardship, fear, sorrow, loneliness and rejection feature in many of them and Bettelheim believed that the exploration of such difficult issues within the safety of the story was helpful since the exploration was symbolic. Take for example the role of the wicked stepmother who appears in so many fairy tales – there are many ideas about why this is the case. Some agree with Bettelheim that it is a way of allowing children to deal with their complicated feelings about their real mothers through the safety of story but also through the device of using the stepmother as surrogate mother.

Many modern fairy tales try to subvert some of the images and messages in older tales. An obvious example is *The Paperbag Princess* by Robert Munsch, where the beautiful princess of traditional tales become a brave and daring character who rejects the weak prince, defeats the dragon and does nothing to be 'princess-like'.

*Folk tales* are the tales of the people. They tell about the rich and the poor, men and women, old and young, brave and foolhardy; they may be humorous or foolish or serious. There are urban legends which, we are told, are the most popular living oral tradition. These are the funny or frightening tales that play on what worries us in the developed world. They might include what are called Tall Stories – stories that are patently not true but may be very entertaining.

*Trickster Tales* are tales where ordinary people – sometimes poor and weak – are tested by fools or devils or fairies. Some cultural heroes are tricksters like Nasreddin Hodja, Ananse, Bre'er Rabbit and others. Here is one of the *Hodja* tales. It is called *The Debt* and it goes like this:

> Nasreddin was strolling through the marketplace when a shopkeeper accosted him, berating the Hodja loudly for his failure to pay a debt. 'My dear friend,' answered the Hodja, 'just how much do I owe you?' 'Seventy-five piasters,' shouted the angry shopkeeper. 'Now, now,' replied the Hodja. 'You must know that I intend to pay you thirty-five piasters tomorrow, and next month another thirty-five. That means that I owe you only five piasters. Are you not ashamed of yourself for accosting me so loudly in public for a debt of only five piasters?'

*Fables*, like those of Aesop, are usually about animals behaving like people and the stories aim to teach young people values, morals and ethics. So they are highly didactic in nature. Here is a translation of one from Nigeria called *Why the Cat Kills Rats*.

> Ansa was King of Calabar for fifty years. He had a very faithful cat as a house-keeper, and a rat was his house-boy. The king was an obstinate, headstrong man, but was very fond of the cat, who had been in his store for many years. The rat, who was very poor, fell in love with one of the king's servant girls, but was unable to give her any presents, as he had no money. At last he thought of the king's store, so in the nighttime, being quite small, he had little difficulty, having made a hole in the roof, in getting into the store. He then stole corn and native pears, and presented them to his sweetheart. At the end of the month, when the cat had to render her account of the things in the store to the king, it was found that a lot of corn and native pears were missing. The king was very angry at this, and asked the cat for an explanation. But the cat could not account for the loss, until one of her friends told her that the rat had been stealing the corn and giving it to the girl. When the cat told the king, he called the

35

girl before him and had her flogged. The rat he handed over to the cat to deal with, and dismissed them both from his service. The cat was so angry at this that she killed and ate the rat, and ever since that time whenever a cat sees a rat she kills and eats it. (Dayrell, 1910, no.18:68-69)

*Nursery tales* are often in verse or song or originate in verse or song and are specifically aimed at young children. Many have cumulative runs where something is added to a sequence. Familiar examples from English folk culture include *The House That Jack Built* or *The Gingerbread Man*. Here is a German version (translated) of a cumulative pancake story. It is called *The Runaway Pancake* and it goes like this:

Two women in Jetzschko were baking a pancake, and when it was almost done they began to quarrel, because each one wanted the whole thing. One woman said, 'I get the pancake!' The other one replied, 'No, I want all of it!' Before they knew what was happening, the pancake suddenly grew feet, jumped out of the pan, and ran away. He came to a fox, who said to him, 'Pancake, pancake, where are you going?' The pancake answered, 'I ran away from two old women, and I shall run away from you as well!' Then he met a hare. It too shouted, 'Pancake, pancake, where are you going?' The pancake answered, 'I ran away from two old women, Reynard the Fox, and I shall run away from you as well. The pancake ran on until he came to some water. A ship full of people was floating on the water. They too cried out to him, 'Pancake, pancake, where are you going?' Again he said, 'I ran away from two old women, Reynard the Fox, Speedy the Hare, and I shall run away from you as well.' Then he came to a large pig. It too shouted to him, 'Pancake, pancake, where are you going?' 'Oh,' he said, 'I ran away from two old women, Reynard the Fox, Speedy the Hare, a ship full of people, and I shall run away from you as well.' The pig said, 'Pancake, I am hard of hearing. You'll have to say it into my ear!' So the pancake went up close, and bam! bam! the pig snatched him and ate him up, and with that the story is ended.

*Creation myths*: These are stories telling of how the world came to be the way it is, why human beings were put into the world and why they die. Creation myths are found in many, many cultures. Here is one example, from The Blackfoot Indians. It is called *The Making of the Earth*.

During the flood, Old Man was sitting on the highest mountain with all the beasts. The flood was caused by the above people, because the baby (a fungus) of the woman who married a star was heedlessly torn in pieces by an Indian child. Old Man sent the Otter down to get some earth. For a long time he waited, then the Otter came up dead. Old Man examined its feet, but found nothing on them. Next he sent Beaver down, but after a long time he also came up drowned. Again nothing was found on his feet. He sent Muskrat to dive next. Muskrat also was drowned. At length he sent the Duck. It was drowned, but in its paw held some earth. Old Man saw it, put it in his hand, feigned putting it on the water three times, and at last dropped it. Then the above-people sent rain, and everything grew on the earth.

There are also many legends, epics, sagas, myths, ballads and songs. Here is a little tale that makes me smile.

There were once five men. The one had no eyes, the second had no legs, the third was dumb, the fourth had no arms, the fifth was naked.
The blind man exclaimed, 'Eh, lads, I see a bird!'
The dumb man said, 'I'll shoot it!'
The man without legs said, 'I'll run after it!'
The man without arms said, 'I'll pick it up!'
And the naked man said, 'I'll put it in my pocket!'
Chorus of Yorkshire children: 'Eh! That is a lie!'
(Baring-Gould, 1866)

## Unravelling the thread

Here is an example of what a child might need to work to make sense of or understand a story, which can be an extremely challenging cognitive task. The African story of *Rabbit at the Water Hole* has parallels in many folk tales around the world. It tells of a great drought in the land and the animals gathering together to decide what to do. With Elephant as Chief they all agreed to dig deep for water. Every animal had to take a turn at digging. After a long day they had dug a deep hole but at the bottom was only a little muddy water. Elephant instructed the animals to leave the water to settle. No-one was to drink until the water was clear. Rabbit was elected to be on guard. Soon tricky Jackal came down to the river and bribed Rabbit with some honey to let him drink some of the water. When the animals returned they found the water muddy and sent Rabbit away in disgrace. Tortoise was elected in his place. Rabbit kept coming back to the water hole because he was getting more and more thirsty. He tried to trick Tortoise but Tortoise was ready for him. He had put bird-lime on his shell and, as you perhaps know, bird-lime is sticky. Finally Rabbit was firmly stuck to Tortoise's shell and the animals decided that Rabbit had to be punished, but Rabbit was so clever that he outwitted them all, ran away and was never seen again.

What, in this story, do the children have to make sense of? They have to understand the importance of water for survival. They have to make sense of the ways in which groups work – perhaps with a chief or a leader who leads the others. They might question why one animal was chosen to play this role. They have to understand why all the animals need to join in digging and why the water at the bottom of the hole needs to be protected. From their own life experience they may well already understand about taking turns and about being tricky. They might identify with Elephant or with tricky Rabbit or with reliable Tortoise. They might admire the way in which Rabbit outwits the others or they may judge him harshly.

Six year old Mzwi said, after hearing this story 'Rabbit is like me – naughty and clever and always in trouble. And Elephant is like my grandma'.

Hannah, who is now 15 years old, asked me if I would like to see the first story she ever told. She made up the story when she was 2 years old and dictated it to an adult who made it into a simple book. It is called *Gemsbok Story*. It is clearly influenced by the story of *Rabbit at the Water Hole*. It goes like this:

> One day there was some gemsbok and they were NASTY, NASTY, NASTY!
>
> One day some elephants came and they wanted to drink their share of the water, but the gemsbok wouldn't let them.
>
> A hyena came to the water hole and drank up all the water.
>
> The elephants found a new water hole and lived happily ever after.

It is a proper story with a beginning and a happy ending (of course!) and told using the language Hannah had encountered in stories she heard read and told. And like all stories, it is rooted in her culture of the time.

## The themes explored

The skilled storyteller can invent a story, re-tell a story or adapt a story to meet any situation, any group of listeners and virtually any theme. Creation myths have been invented in various cultures to explain how the world and the things in it came to be. Fables came about so that the values and morals of a culture could be passed on from generation to generation. Things that baffle people – like fairness and equity, class structures, weakness and strength – are explored through tales like *The Princess and the Pea* where royalty is so sensitive it can detect a pea beneath piles of mattresses, or *Jack and the Beanstalk* where a small child outwits a giant or the story of *Rabbit at the Waterhole*.

Many traditional tales explore things that worry children like wicked stepmothers, being abandoned, going hungry or not fitting in.

## The child's work

Children work hard to make sense of the world by looking and listening, touching and moving, mimicking and inventing, making rules and changing them. They do all this primarily through their play and by structuring their own thoughts , feelings and experiences into little stories or protonarratives.

They hear stories all the time, at home, at school, in the playground, on television, and in books. Their lives are full of narratives – some about everyday events, some about the past and some even about unknown places, people and events. What they have to do is listen, memorise, and make meaning. The stories they hear may be in everyday language, when for example, they hear about what happened during the day. 'I had a dreadful day' says mum 'It just didn't stop raining and the baby kept crying and the shops were crowded'. They may be playground tales like ''Munir went to tell the teacher that you were calling me names'. They may be stories told more formally as part of the cultural rituals of their community or fantastical stories told in books or on television. As children listen they learn that one of the ways of making sense of the world and the people in it is to shape it into a narrative.

Stories, like language, are rule-bound. Meek (1988) calls storytelling a kind of game with rules. It is universal and particularly human. Cultures have are particular ways of starting a story. Many English stories begin with 'Once upon a time' and end with 'lived happily ever after'. In Trinidad and some French Caribbean islands a storyteller traditionally invites an audience to a storytelling session by asking 'Cric?' to which the response of 'Crac' implies acceptance. There is convention around storytelling common among the Inuit people in Alaska. Most commonly it is the young girls aged between of 6 and 12 who become storytellers. They are often accompanied by 'tagalongs' – younger siblings who sit and watch and are inducted into the rules of what deMarrais *et al* (1994) call 'meaning-making in mud.' Here storytelling is seen as a vital part of retaining kinship patterns, reinforcing gender roles, building the oral tradition and maintaining cultural norms and values. It is seen as a vital part of learning, as we can see from how the young learners use observation, spatial relationships, sequencing, classifying, predicting, solving problems and memory skills. The storyteller has to tell and illustrate her story and does this by pressing a dull, flat knife into the mud to make marks as she speaks. Each mark is erased and replaced by a new mark in a ritual known as storyknifing.

The children learn about the language of narrative – how it can be used in a straightforward way as when telling everyday events – or in more poetic, repetitive ways in group storytelling or storyreading events. As they become increasingly experienced story tellers, which, crucially involves them hearing more and more stories and stories of different types, they begin to include story language in their tales. Here are some examples drawn from the wonderful work of Vivian Gussin Paley.

First, here is Mollie putting her Barbie doll to sleep

> 'Sh-sh baby sleepy go to sleepy are you asleep or are you silly? Little wind blowing see how I blow? Do you see me or do you want anything I have? Mmm will you sleep mmm oh sleep oh sleep mmm to sleep good little baby I love you sweetheart'. (Paley, 1988:74)

This is not the language of great literature but it is also not Mollie's everyday language. She is drawing on lullabies, the songs she has heard, the lilt in the voice of someone putting a baby to sleep

Next is Angie, whose story goes like this:

> 'Once there was a unicorn and butterflies... They played all day in the meadow... Then one day a monster ate up the unicorn. But she kicked at him and he ran away. The end.' (Paley, 1988:94)

Here is a perfect little story with a traditional beginning, a series of events, a set of characters and a double ending, first tragic, but then changed to make it happy. In her daily speech Angie would never start a sentence with 'Once there was' or end one with 'the end'.

From hearing stories, children learn a great deal about their own culture and its traditions and values and symbols. They learn about people and the reasons for their actions, about here and now and long ago and about possible and imagined worlds.

Listening to a story and engaging with it might seem merely pleasurable and not intellectually demanding, but in reality it presents the child with enormous cognitive challenges. Meek (1991) tells us that from the stories we hear as children we 'inherit the ways in which we talk about how we feel, the values which we hold to be important and what we regard as the truth' (p103).

## Building a culture and pedagogy based on narrative

■ To help the children in your care become effective listeners to stories and makers of their own stories you can do nothing better than become a storyteller yourself. You may well be one of the many fine natural storytellers who are able to tell stories about everyday events, stories you have learnt yourself and stories you have invented. But most of us find telling stories much harder than reading them because we feel so exposed by not having the prop of a book in our hands to guide us through. But I urge you to learn to do this. As you tell the stories you can watch children and respond to their responses. It becomes a dialogic process which is really rewarding once you get over your initial nervousness. Start with a simple familiar tale and tell it rather than read it. Practice at home first or with a friend. After doing it once you will find it easier and easier to do.

■ Become familiar with many stories. There are wonderful collections around, some of which are cited at the end of the book. Try and find tales relating to the lives, cultures and languages of the children in your group. Ask parents and others in the community if they know tales you can learn.

■ You can make the events of your life into a story. When my younger daughter fell off a borrowed bicycle whilst staying with a friend in the country and was left lying in the road while the friend went for help, I told the story to the children I was teaching. They were totally silent through-out the telling and for weeks would come and ask me how she was. They could identify with her and make links between her experience and feel-ings and their own.

■ It you feel completely unable to become a storyteller yourself, try and find storytellers, professional and other, who might come into your class or setting to tell stories to the children. Parents or grandparents might be willing to come in and tell stories and you can find professional story-tellers online at these websites www.the-storytellers.com/; www.sfs.org.uk/; www.scottishstorytellingcentre.co.uk/; www.cambridgestorytellers.com; www.xanthegresham.co.uk/; www.crickcrackclub.com/; www.just imaginestorycentre.cl.uk/or through your library or community centre.

■ Make links with a theatre if you can find one in your vicinity and devise ways of working with them. Some theatre groups will come into schools or settings to work with children. Visiting a theatre is another way for chil-dren to make meaning through what they have seen and heard.

# 4

## Reading the images

Closing my eyes I see palm trees swaying.
Seagulls circling. Haciendas, pink and green.
(From *Mi Mamma Cubana* by Mimi Chapra)

In this chapter we turn our attention to a relatively new and distinct genre of children's literature – the wordless picturebook. What does the artist/ narrator do to draw the child into a world made by the pictures and to create a story which is not fixed but fluid, open to interpretation and able to reflect aspects of the individual child's experience and feelings? Note that the books are not completely wordless: all have a title, the name of the artist and sometimes a dedication or words within the pictures, such as shop names, signs and so on. Rowe (1996:221) suggests that these books might well be labelled 'sequenced picture texts'.

There are two extremes when we consider the relationship between word and picture. At one extreme is the pictureless text and at the other the wordless picturebook. Both can be divided into the narrative and the non-narrative. There are many picturebooks, called exhibit books, which invite children to name objects or colours or count the images on a page. A picture dictionary is one such wordless exhibit book. Then there are books where the illustrations carry the narrative alone. These are the wordless picturebooks which are the focus for this chapter.

### Looking at wordless picturebooks

Wordless picturebooks abound and you may well be familiar with some of them – the books of Jan Ormerod and Mitsumasa Anno and *The Snowman* by Raymond Briggs, which in turn became a wordless film and a wordless play. In books like these it is the sequence of the images that invite the child to create the narrative or tell the story. We start by looking in some detail at a recent wordless picturebook with a view to thinking about what it is that the artist – who is also the silent narrator – is doing.

The book is *Wave* by Suzy Lee. This beautiful and seemingly simple book is rectangular, rather like setting up a page in landscape format, which allows for the artist to give the illusion of a long beach. The colours are muted – greys and blacks and the wonderful blue of the sea. A little girl and her mother come down to the beach. Five gulls fly overhead. The girl dances on the beach, ventures tentatively close to the sea, backs away, goes closer still. The expression on her face changes. It is only when she is knocked down by a wave and then discovers the treasures the wave brings with it that she starts to feel excited rather than frightened. Despite the lack of words on the page there is the clear sense of a dialogue between the child and the wave. At the end the child and mother leave the beach and the child turns to wave to her friend, the wave.

How do the pictures work and what has the artist had to consider in creating the images? Suzy Lee was born in Seoul, Korea and lives in Singapore. She first studied art in Korea but subsequently did an MA in Book Arts at the Camberwell College of Arts in London. She has been awarded many prizes for her books including the Best Illustrated Children's Book Award in 2008 for *Wave*. Suzy has one small child (to whom *Wave* is dedicated) and is pregnant with the next. She says that, as a child, she had a book *The Shrinking of Treehorn* by Florence Heide with strange drawings by Edward Gorey. She read it again and again to try and figure out what it was about and she liked the feeling of the strange and mysterious. She says she starts her books with something fairly basic that interests her – perhaps a shape or a colour. This then becomes the key image of the story. In *Wave* the curl of the wave, the circularity of the child and the birds and the intense blue of the water are essential themes. The story that emerges is fluid, open to interpretation and able to be adopted by any child. The book itself is a piece of art. This is not surprising in light of the knowledge that she is a book artist.

## Making a wordless picturebook

Those making wordless picturebooks use a range of devices and strategies to draw the viewer into the unfolding narrative. These include considerations of the following:

- how to frame the images
- how to sequence the events

- the movement of figures on the page
- the direction of figures and events across the pages
- how pictures act as signs
- how to allow the viewer to draw on prior experience

The first recorded wordless picturebook, published in 1968, is *Vikki* by Renate Meyer, the story of a friendless little girl who knits herself a friend. The book was negatively reviewed when it appeared. People said that a book without words could not be described as a book. How could such a book be read? We now know that we read much more than words. We read everything we encounter in our attempts to make sense of the world and everything in it. So we read pictures – which is a cognitively challenging act of creating a narrative, sustaining the narrative and adapting it to meet our own needs and feelings. It seems clear that the ways in which we interpret what we see and how we structure that into a narrative largely depends on what we have seen and done. What is more, each time we open the book or watch the film we, the observers, watchers or beholders, can change the tale we tell. Unlike the words on the page which are fixed, the images are fluid in the sense of being open to interpretation.

The narrators/artists work within four traditions: art history, film language, media images and book making. We touched on the impact of studying book making in looking at Suzy Lee's work and now consider how the language of film has influenced the making of wordless picturebooks. Film makers must make decisions about whether to use a long shot or a close up, what angle to film at and *how to frame the images*. We see the influence of this in certain picturebooks. In Maurice Sendak's *Where the Wild Things Are* there are both words and images and the author and artist are the same person. There are double-spread unframed pictures where the rumpus takes place and there is no need for words. Sendak uses the device of presenting the most active and dream-like and potentially frightening events without words to draw the reader in. Suzy Lee uses the device of spreading every image over two pages to give the double the length of the beach.

Some books use the fractured page: the page is broken up into smaller and often different sized boxes which provide runs of sequences. In Shaun Tan's *The Red Book* the fractured page is used to great effect.The reason for it is not always clear at first glance and requires close looking and possibly discussion. In Tan's wonderful wordless picturebook for older children *The Arrival* you can clearly see the influence of film and graphic novels and comics.

The *sequence of events* is always key to the narrative. In wordless picturebooks the artist has to allow the child reader to make sense of what happens at the beginning, what happens next and how that affects what comes afterwards. In the absence of words the pictures provide clues of sequence although there is still some fluidity which allows the child to interpret. The child determines a beginning and an end and possibly everything that happens in between.

Playing with the layout of a book is a device often used by artists of children's books. Suzy Lee's most recent book, *Shadows*, does this very effectively, enabling the young reader to explore the properties of books as well as allowing the narrative to change along with the orientation of the book itself. *Shadows* is about a little girl playing in the attic where she finds a ladder, a pair of old shoes, a broom and a bike. Each casts a shadow on the page below. After seeing the book and exploring it, the child reader will learn to hold the book with the spine parallel to her eye line. This allows for a top and a bottom page: the items on the top and the shadows of the items on the bottom. The little girl in the book makes her fingers take the shape of a bird, puts the shoe on her head to become a pretend wolf and, as she carries on playing, the shadows come to life and transform into other things. The seam separating the two pages now seems to become the barrier between the real world and the imaginary world. This is an interesting feature of some books and can be defined as a *metafictive device*. It is a way for the artist, in this case, to draw the child reader's attention to the fact that what she is playing with or looking at is a book. This raises questions about what is real and what is fiction or narrative. In Lee's book the shadows realise what has happened and the shoe-wolf leaps over the seam separating the pages, thus leaving the imaginary world for the real world and the little girl has to be rescued by the finger-bird. If the book is rotated the shadows can be at the top with the little girl below, opening up a whole new thread of possible narratives.

Artists also pay attention to *movement*. Many of the wordless picturebooks have implied movement in them as the main character goes on some sort of journey, physical or imagined or dreamlike or magical. The hen goes for a walk through a farmyard in *Rosie's Walk*; Max sails away on a journey in *Where the Wild Things Are* – or does he? In *Waves* the child goes to the beach where she begins a sort of dance with the water. Julia Donaldson's *The Gruffalo* tells of the journey of a mouse who strolls into the *deep dark wood*, reassured that there is no such thing as a Gruffalo. But, of course, he encounters the creature with its *knobbly knees and turned out toes, And a poisonous wart on the end of his nose*. On the journey many things may be encountered – objects, people, places, sensations, feeling, thoughts – some frightening or funny or strange. Then there is an ending where it is all resolved.

Artists play with movement in another sense. In almost all children's picture-books *movement proceeds from left to right* – in the direction of English print across the page. In *Rosie's Walk* the hen plods steadfastly around the farmyard across each of the page-openings from left to right, thus inviting us to turn the page. The same things happens when Max sails off in his boat. It is only when he returns home that the direction is reversed. This left to right direction operates in almost all of the books mentioned in this chapter and the next. There is one notable and exciting exception. In *The Park in the Dark* three toys are left abandoned in the park at night and are frightened when they see a passing train going from right to left. They rush away from the park towards the left-hand edge of the book, back home.

In wordless picturebooks the *images themselves are visual signs* to which the child reader must assign meaning, drawing on her own experiences, perspectives and contexts. This is important because it reminds us that reading – reading of anything – means making meaning. Artists/narrators help their young readers use the signs on the page to construct narrative. In *Rosie's Walk* the main character is a hen named Rosie who goes for a walk on a farm. Behind her and unseen by her is a fox. As Rosie walks she inadvertently does things that cause harm to the fox. She arrives home in time for dinner, quite unaware that most of the way she had been accompanied by a fox. It is helpful to think about what is this narrative about. Is it aimed at teaching children about what might be found on a farm? Or is it about how a small creature (like a hen or a child) can outwit something dangerous like a fox?

Meek considers *Rosie's Walk* to be a classic story with a beginning, a middle and an end. Each double-spread page constitutes an episode, labelled with a three word positional text such as 'over the haycock' or '*through* the fence'. The child reads the pictures, the adult reads the words, the child constructs the narrative. This is a polysemic text. It uses more than one way of signifying meaning. Pat Hutchins in this, her first book, set out to engage the interest of all young children, not only those familiar with farms. Her pictures are de-tailed and patterned and she is clever at making her images take the reader, effortlessly, from page to page so they feel they are accompanying Rosie on her walk. Most children will have had experience of going for a walk, of look-ing around, of getting home in time for dinner, of doing something surprising and of jokes and humour. And the book is full of visual and implied jokes. Bakhtin (1981) said that laughter has the remarkable power of making an object come up close, of drawing it into a zone of crude contact where one can finger it familiarly on all sides, turn it upside down, inside out, peer at it from above and below, break open its external shell, look into its center, doubt it, take it apart, dismember it, lay it bare and expose it, examine it freely and experiment with it. Laughter demolishes fear and piety before an object, before a world, making of it an object of familiar contact and thus clearing the ground for an absolutely free investigation of it... Familiarization of the world through laughter and popular speech is an extremely important and indispensable step in making possible free, scientifically knowable and artistically realistic creativity in European civilization. (p23)

One of the things artist/narrators do is to try and *find things that are universal enough to allow most children draw on their previous experience* in making sense of the narrative.

Wordless or nearly wordless narratives take place in books but also in films. In the recent film *Wall*E* who is a little robot Wall*E is cleaning up the earth all by himself. The earth had been badly polluted and then abandoned by humans hundreds of years ago. Wall*E has spent his time examining the refuse of the humans and through this has thought of and felt many things. Some of these are tested when a spaceship arrives carrying a scanning robot called EVE. You have guessed what happens next. Smitten, he follows her to where the last surviving humans live and tries to teach them about love and responsibility. The film was made by Pixar, who decided to reduce most of the film to a dialogue-free pantomime which leaves it to the beholder to create the story from the moving images on screen.

## Who are wordless picturebooks designed for?

Wordless picturebooks are often thought of as being for only very young children but in reality they are often also of interest to older children and certainly to children who may not yet be fluent in English. The most inventive and imaginative examples of wordless picturebooks are of interest to adults too. To illustrate this here are the responses of different people to *Wave*:

■ Liliana is nearly 4 years old. She has had encounters with many books and stories at home because her mother is a teacher and her father a journalist and the house is full of books. When she was given a copy of *Wave* she spent a long time turning the pages and looking intently at each image. This is her accompanying monologue:

> No words. No words. Is it a book? It is a book. She is with her mum on the beach and there's birds. And the sea is blue and wavy. She looks a little

scared. I went to the beach. I found shells. Look, here's shells. She loves the shells. I love my shells. The wave dropped the shells for her. Now she's going home with her mum and she is waving goodbye.

■ Rifat is 7 years old and has only been in this country for a few months. He is learning English but is not confident about speaking it. He too looked at the book with great interest, turning the pages. He went back to the book day after day, his teacher said. And after about a week he brought it to the teacher and said 'Sea ... boat. Me in boat come London'.

■ Eric said 'I first encountered *Wave* when I was on a book making course. We had been talking about the work of book artists who produce books as things of beauty rather than narrative. I found the book to be both. I was mesmerised by the beauty of the images, the format and the possibilities of narrative the book suggested to me.'

■ Ameeta, aged 5, looked at the pictures three times in a row without saying anything. But she finally turned to the adult with her and said 'Inside front different. Look, no shells and pretty blue things'. The adult, intrigued, returned to look again at the book and realised that this small child had noticed that the endpapers at the front were different from those at the back of the book. The child had paid closer attention to the visual images than the adult had.

One book can say different things to people according to their own experiences. Jude, who is an advisory teacher, looked at *Wave* and asked me how I would respond to a small children saying 'I've got pink shoes' whilst looking at the book. There is no clear prompt for such a statement in the pictures or the narrative. I had to think hard about this but finally decided that perhaps the child had noticed that the girl in the book was not wearing any shoes at all. Her own new pink shoes were clearly important to her and perhaps the sight of those bare feet had given her the opportunity to make this link with her own experience. So she used this as the starting point of a whole new conversation. Encountering a response from a child which is initially baffling and seems unrelated to what is happening in the classroom or setting is not unusual. Finding out as much as possible about the child's experience helps decode and contextualise such responses. The response of the adult will give the child some indication of how carefully adults take account of what she is doing and saying.

I am often asked which age group a book is designed or suitable for and I find this almost impossible to answer. Yet the question is asked in bookshops and libraries or of teachers or parents. A book is for someone to whom it speaks. A very young child may be interested in aspects of complex stories or an adult interested in the seeming simplicity of wordless picturebooks.

There is an apocryphal story about a little girl who fell in love with books and stories and could read when she started school. The reception class teacher gave her primer after primer and the child became more and more introverted and unhappy at school. Eventually the mother was called in so the teacher could tell her her concerns. The teacher told the mother that the child clearly had special needs because she never talked at school. The mother went to fetch her daughter from the classroom and together they confronted the class teacher and the headteacher. The mother turned to the little girl and said 'For goodness sake, Nicola, say something. They think you are stupid because you don't talk. You have to say something'. After a pause Nicola said 'Can I say anything, mum, or does it have to be relevant?'

All children are individuals and will have individual and personal responses. Some will read surprisingly complex books, others will not. It rarely depends on age.

## The significance of pictures

To communicate and share our ideas, thoughts and feelings about the world we have developed and used signs and symbols in our communicative systems. The ways of communicating change the way we think. A book read or a film seen may have long term effects on thinking. A film is made up of moving visual images (signs) and a book is made of words (symbols). Vygotsky called the ways of communication human being have developed 'cultural tools'. They allow us to think about things even when they are no longer present. So the child developing a narrative through looking at images will be able to remember parts of the narrative after the book is closed. There is a link between thinking and cultural tools and memory. Vygotsky talked about mediation – how cultural tools bring about changes in thinking. The intention of the book maker – artist or illustrator or author – is to convey ideas, thoughts, messages and feelings to the beholder or reader. So the artist uses still images in paint, chalk, crayon, ink or pen to create a sequence and the child looking at the images makes sense of them by constructing a narrative from them. A film maker uses moving images to achieve the same thing. An author uses the symbolic format of words to structure and share meaning.

The task for the viewer or beholder of a wordless picturebook is to use the sequence of still images to construct a narrative and the narrative thus con-

structed will depend on the experience, ideas, thoughts and needs of the beholder. Where the pictures simply illustrate a story presented in words the
role of the child reader is to relate to the narrative, but not necessarily to
construct it. Where the child is reading the words the pictures may provide
helpful clues to the text. This is an aid often used by beginning readers. Where
there are no pictures the reader is dependent on decoding the symbolic (the
letters and words) into the meaningful (the narrative/meaning).

Crawford and Hade (2000) carried out research to try and see what strategies
children of different ages and book experience used in making sense of wordless texts. They focused on three children, 8 year old Laura, 5 year old Tim and
4 year old Arlee. Laura and Tim are siblings and attend a school where books
have high status. Arlee does not yet attend school. All three are privileged children. Each child was offered twelve different wordless picturebooks to
explore and then asked choose one to read or tell aloud. This process was
repeated so that ultimately each child had the opportunity to read and talk
about three different books. The researchers first analysed the children's
choice of book and found that the visual impact of the book cover played a
part for two of the children. Arlee chose Tomie de Paolo's *Pancakes for Breakfast* because he liked the look of the pancakes. Tim chose Jan Ormerod's
*Moonlight* but rejected the same artist's *Sunshine* on the basis that this was a
'girl's book 'because of the image of a girl in her nightgown on the back cover.
Laura, the oldest of the three, chose Ward's *The Silver Pony* because its thick-
ness – another physical characteristic of the book – suggested that it would be
a longer book.

The researchers then explored the relationships between making sense of the
books with prior experience, experience of other books or texts, being able to
see things from the perspective of different characters, experience of story
language and story rituals and active or playful exploration. This is what they
found:

### Making sense using prior knowledge and learning

For all three children there was evidence that their prior knowledge and
learning played a part in their ability to make sense of wordless books. Arlee,
the youngest, asked the adults to read the title and the dedication and then
spent time looking for the words. 'Where are the words? ... I got words in my
books'. He explicitly refers to his previous experience of books having words
in them. The two older children were less surprised to encounter no words. It
emerged that they had had some experience of reading wordless books.

### Making sense using intertextuality

Many books exploit *intertextuality* or making reference to other books and texts. All three children made reference to other books when making their choices. Laura justified her choice with reference to the particular characteristics of other books she had enjoyed. Interestingly all children also made reference to other texts – namely those on television, films or other media.

### Making sense through taking multiple perspectives

Arlee was able to make sense of *Pancakes for Breakfast* through being able to move back and forth between his first person perspective inside the picture and the more remote third-person perspective outside the frame. So he shifted between talking about 'I' and 'she' or 'he'. The older children consistently told the stories from outside the frame, but, by supplying dialogue, indicated that they could also become the character within the frame.

### Making sense through familiarity with language and story rituals

All three children revealed awareness of the story rituals in their culture. Stories had beginnings and endings and the language used was often, although not always, that of books – as where Tim used phrases like 'as he comes back out with his friends' which is clearly the sort of phrase to be found in books rather than in the everyday language of the home or classroom.

### Making sense through playful behaviours

The children in the study often used playful behaviours by basing the story on their play or their play on the story. They introduced sound effects, funny voices , gestures or facial expressions. Laura formally introduced the stories she was telling. Tim, however, rarely did this and he often broke the story frame to offer his opinion.

## The themes explored

Wordless picturebooks are predominantly open-ended but it is clear that through the images on the page they can be highly culture-specific. On a recent visit to a well-respected bookshop in North London I was extremely distressed to find just how prevalent the dominance of one culture over others can be. This bookshop has an excellent children's section and on a large display rack were wonderful wordless and other picturebooks in many shapes and sizes, featuring fantastic illustrations. But there was not a single face on the cover of any of the books that was not white or that of some animal or creature. Behind the main rack and set back from view was a smaller rack on which were displayed about ten books with the faces of brown or black children on them. Children make the stories from the pictures. Where the pictures are thus culturally limited so also are the opportunities for children to engage with them. Some illustrators take care to make the images more general so that a child could be black or white, male or female.

Although the artist to some extent determines the theme of the wordless picturebook it is up to the child to make the book her own. Remember the example of the mythical small child talking about pink shoes when looking at *Wave?* Her interest was related, perhaps, to new shoes, or much desired shoes. Another child might have made up a story about overcoming a fear or never having been to the seaside or only have a mum and no dad or wishing to have a brother or sister.

## The child's work

Children spent much of their time trying to understand their world and the people in it. To do so they have to infer meaning from different sources. Initially, as they look, listen, touch and move they notice many things. They notice that the faces of the people around them change. Mum's mouth sometimes turns up at the edges and sometimes down. People's voices change too: dad's voice can be soft and tickly in the ear or loud and scary. From all their experience they begin to attribute meaning to the changes they encounter. This involves them in many complex cognitive tasks. First is memory. In order to notice change there has to be a memory of the thing before it changed. Then there is comparison: what is different? Then there is purpose, the big question: why? Why do people's expressions and voices change? Why are some days bright and sunny and others dark and wet? Children begin to attribute motives and reasons for the things they notice.

In *Wave* all the child sees on the pages is a barefoot child on a beach, five birds, the water and mum in the background. The artist has only the child's face and body to tell the reader that it is the same child on each page, feeling or experiencing something different on each. On the title page the smiling child is running towards the water, with her mother following behind. On the next page she stands, alone, at the water's edge with her hands behind her back, looking at the water. The five birds line up behind her. On the next page a little wave splashes down in front of her and she is shown running away and looking back at it. This time the birds are running ahead of her, away from the sea. On the following page she has turned back to the sea, standing on tiptoe with her hands raised above her head and her mouth wide open in a shout. The birds, behind her, flap their wings at the noise. And so on.

This is the beginning of the story 4 year old Elsie told as she leafed through the book. 'She's going to the beach and she is happy. Oh, she is looking at the water and now a wave comes and she is a little scared. Now, look, she is trying to scare the water. She is shouting at it...' For the child to have created such a narrative she has to have understood that there is only one child in the story and that she is feeling different things as she interacts with the wave. Elsie has to infer all of this from the images and the sequence and does so by drawing on her own experience of having made or witnessed the expressions and movements portrayed in the images.

When invited to look at a wordless picturebook children examine the sequence of pictures by turning the pages and may come to find the essence of a story. There is a starting point – the cover of the book with its picture, title and name of the artist and then the first page where something begins to happen. If this interests the child she may turn the page to see what happens next and on and on until there is an ending. So the child needs to turn the pages in the sequence that applies to the language of the book – conventionally from left to right for English and European languages; from right to left for languages such as Arabic and Hebrew. Then the child needs to pay really close attention to the images to make sense of them and work out what is happening in them. From this the child begins to construct the sequence where one thing follows another. And thus the narrative grows. It may well be a slow process and adults looking at a book with the child need to be patient and to hand control over to the child.

## Building a culture and pedagogy based on narrative

- Be patient. Allow the child time to look at the pictures. Only intervene if invited by the child and only ask a question if it is directly related to what you think the child is paying attention to. Remember it is up to the child to read the pictures in order to create a story. Wordless picturebooks are open-ended, allowing the beholder to become the narrator and to change the narration with each telling.

- These books are really for use by a single child or a pair or small group of children. They are not suitable for using with a big group because the children need close access so they can pore over the pictures and choose when to move on.

- Try to offer a good selection of such books, chosen precisely because they are open-ended, attractive and carry hidden narratives. Spend time getting to know the wide range of these books and select them carefully because many are expensive and some are 'better' than others. This is a value judgement only in the sense of reminding you to look for books that allow for narrative making. If you offer children books which invite them to name objects you are not thinking about the narrative possibilities in them.

- Remember that wordless picturebooks are as accessible to children with little or no English as to those for whom English is their first language.

- Become familiar with any book you propose using. That means having a look at it before you offer it to a child. I found that *The Red Book*, although recommended for young children, was too complex and multilayered for young children to make sense of.

- Learn from the children. You may well find that very young children are better at reading pictures than adults are and find creating a narrative a more natural thing to do. We, as adults, have had years of reading text to overlay our reading of pictures.

# 5

## The interweaving of
## pictures with words

...it isn't hard for me to remember that time in our lives when I lived without
yesterday or tomorrow and Grandma served heaven on a spoon. (*Look*, 1999.
Author's Note)

This chapter moves from looking at artists making wordless picturebooks to the author and artist working collaboratively to create early
picturebooks where the picture and the words both carry the story.
Some of the most admired picturebooks have been made by one person who
is both artist and author, such as Eric Carle, Maurice Sendak and Anthony
Browne. The features of these books differ from those of wordless books since
their creators have to consider how to make the narrative in words and pictures both work, either to tell the same story, although not necessarily the
identical story, or to tell parallel stories. The creators also need to think about
how they can encourage the young reader to engage in more and more complex interactions with the book, going from constructing a narrative from the
pictures, to memorising the narrative well enough to be able to re-tell the
story using the pictures and textual cues, to finding things in the pictures and
words which allow them to draw on their own experience and eventually become not only an independent reader but a lover of books and narrative.

Thus books like these, with their often conscious exploitation of aspects of
print, play a much more obvious role in children becoming readers. The presence of words on the page make the story fixed. Many of you will be familiar
with how quickly children realise this and point out when you try to skip a few
lines. As active meaning makers even very young children come to realise that
it is the words on the page which carry the narrative and also ensure that what

57

they hear when the words are read aloud is the same on every occasion. This has obvious implications for their becoming not only readers but also narrators and then writers. Many children continue to read the narrative carried by the pictures too, which may be an elaboration on the words or, as in Anthony Browne's work, for example, a different parallel text.

The makers of these books often have in mind the implied child reader alongside an adult or more expert reader. The text will often be minimal, designed to be memorable and full of features used specifically to scaffold young children becoming independent readers.

## Features of early written text that help children become independent readers

There is something about the *language of books and stories* which draws the reader or the listener into the world of the narrative. We saw how Hannah could remember long, complex and sometimes meaningless lines of nonsense rhymes because the sounds and rhythms pleased her. An author who skillfully uses language itself to great effect is Julia Donaldson. Her description of the creature, *the Gruffalo*, immediately excites the imagination of the reader. A thing with terrible tusks and terrible claws and terrible teeth in his terrible jaws, with orange eyes and black tongue and purple prickles – what could be more vivid? She uses rhyme and repetition and rhythm, and the adult reading the book aloud almost sings the melody of the words. The structure of the language makes it so easy that the reader can almost literally lift the tune from the page. At the heart of the book is the serious issue of danger and how we come to know who or what is dangerous and how to handle this.

Underpinning the whole book is the *unspoken dialogue between the adult reader and the child listener*. Michael Rosen, writing in the *The Guardian* (9 June 2011) says that the implication of this is that the child continually and silently asks 'can you protect me and keep me safe?' to which the adult continually silently responds 'Yes, I am strong and big enough to always keep you from harm'. This pinpoints another important feature of the potential power of literature: the dialogue set up between the reader and the listener around the themes of the book and the child's relationship to them.

*'Ahhh!' Said Stork* by Gerald Rose is the story of a stork who finds a bird, wants to eat it, but cannot crack the shell. There are few words on each page. A procession of animals try in various ways to crack the egg, with no success. The animals stop and gather together to think. Finally the egg cracks by itself and out comes a baby crocodile, who gleefully proclaims he will get revenge when

he is big enough. On each of eight brilliantly coloured double- page spreads we find an animal doing something to the egg as where the text reads, for example 'Hippopotamus rolled on it' and where the action is described in words but also made absolutely clear through the pictures. The emphasis in the book is on the verbs. Actions are easy to illustrate.

Some writers, like Kornei Chukovsky (1963), think that verbs are the words most likely to hold the interest of young children in light of their growing physical skills. The text is fuller on the final pages. A child will very quickly be able to 'read' almost all of the text through reading the pictures and remembering the pattern since there is clear *repetition of the pattern* of text from page to page.

Some authors use the technique of using a *repeated refrain* to which something is added each time the refrain occurs. A variation of this takes place in *Mr Gumpy's Outing* by John Burningham. Mr Gumpy agrees to take two children and some animals on a journey in his boat on condition that each agrees to behave according to the rules Mr Gumpy sets. Burningham is reminding the reader that some behaviours are acceptable in certain contexts or cultures. The text forms a cumulative story: it builds up , step by step, page turn by page turn, animal by animal, condition by condition. It is worth telling you that I did not notice how the text changed, nor did I think about why until I read Meek's seminal text *How Texts Teach What Readers Learn*. It is worth quoting some of the text to actually see how Burningham manages this:

> May we come with you? said the children.
> Yes', said Mr Gumpy,
> 'if you don't squabble'...
> 'Can I come along, Mr Gumpy?' said the rabbit.
> 'Yes, but don't hop about'
> 'Have you a place for me?' said the sheep.
> 'Yes, but don't keep bleating...
> 'Can you make room for me? said the calf.
> 'Yes, if you don't trample about...
> 'May I join you, Mr Gumpy?' said the goat.
> 'Very well, but don't kick'.

Notice that each of these is essentially the same request, but slightly differently phrased. What Burningham does here is illustrate the different ways in which a request can be made.

What about the text below?

'May I come, please, Mr Gumpy? said the pig.

'Very well, but don't muck about'.

'Can we come too? said the chickens.

'Yes, but don't flap!

Burningham is offering his young readers ways of asking and answering questions, using the device of keeping the meaning the same but varying the form. In this way he extends the ways in which questions can be asked and answered. But he also plays with words and their meanings; 'don't muck about' and don't flap' can mean different things. And in the context in which he uses the phrases he makes the words mean more than they say.

Many writers for young children use *metaphor*: one thing stands for or represents another through some implied or stated comparison. To understand metaphor the child must be able to compare one thing with another to find what is the same and what different. The linguistic device of simile also compares one thing to another but the comparison is direct rather than implied. Sendak in his wonderfully terrifying book *Outside Over There* uses direct comparison when he says things like 'Oh how those goblins hollered and kicked, just babies like her sister' which is easy for children to comprehend. But when the goblins come to kidnap the baby and the little girl, Ida, finds in his place a baby made of ice, the comparison is indirect and allows for much speculation, thought and discussion. Ida, jealous of the baby and angry about having to care for him, finds him gone and then has to deal with her complex feelings of fear, sorrow and shame. So the device of using metaphor allows young children to make connections they might not otherwise have been able to make. It is a very powerful suggestive tool.

Another story with a *repeated refrain* is *Peace at Last* by Jill Murphy. Poor Mr Bear can't get to sleep because of the noises, human, animal and other, which cause him to cry out in despair. 'Oh NO!' said Mr Bear 'I can't stand THIS' is his repeated refrain throughout the book as noise keeps him from sleeping wherever he goes. This repeated refrain invites children to join in. At William Patten Infants School many years ago, the reception class had a teacher called Pritha and the class made a book about the things they did which made their teacher cry out the same thing as Mr Bear. So on one page of the book it reads 'Rifat slammed the door. 'Oh NO!' said Pritha 'I can't stand THIS'; on the next page 'Annabelle dropped the pens. 'Oh NO!' said Pritha 'I can't stand THIS' and so on.

Just as in wordless picturebooks the pictures in early picturebooks are carefully framed and sequenced and laid out on the page but here *the placing and design of the text* also play a part in attracting and holding children's interest and drawing them into the magic of story. In *The Odd Egg* by Emily Gravett (2009) the author is also the artist and she uses text, pictures and layout in an unusual way. The first page of the book shows one feather; the second a duck and a feather, the third a feather high in the air. The narrative text only starts on the sixth page, where we learn that all the birds have laid an egg except for Duck and we see a bird reading a book called 'The Bright Baby Book'. So here we find a book within a book. Text also appears at the base of a prize-winning egg trophy and in another book, 'Egg Spotters Guide', and in the mocking sounds of the other birds. Finally, on a series of cut down pages, text describes the noises made by the cracking eggs and the reactions of the watching birds, which range range from tweet to the humorous algebraic formula of the naturally wise baby owl who tweets algebraically! Later, as Duck waits for his egg to hatch Gravett uses suspense: 'he waited ... and waited ... and then SNAP!' as the surprise emerges from the egg.

Sally Grindley wrote her own version of the *Jack and the Beanstalk* story in a book called '*Shhh*' and invited Peter Utton to illustrate it. The device she focused on was to keep reminding the reader that everything that was happening was within the safety of the book. The object is to get through the book, room by room, or page by page, without waking the sleeping giant. Throughout the book the reader is invited to look back through the windows on the page to make sure the giant is still asleep. Inevitably the reader wakes the sleeping giant and the only way of dealing with it is to shut the book quickly to escape. This book makes the child aware that this is a book and that closing it makes the scary thing go away. It uses *metafiction* (the skill of re-minding the reader throughout that what is being read is a book) to great effect.

This is what some nursery children said after having the book read to them, three times in a row, by popular request:

Judit: I was so scared. I kept putting my hands over my ears, but then I wanted to hear what was next.

Henry: Every time the teacher said 'Shh' I joined in and so did my friends.

Elliott: I went up to look backwards and check he was still asleep

Nameeda: I was so scared when the giant woke up, I shouted.

Aram: When the teacher shut the book we all laughed and said 'Again! again!

And when the nursery teacher asked the children why they wanted to hear it again and again, one child said 'It was a safe scary book.'

In *Hide and Snake*, written and illustrated in vivid acrylics and wonderful design by Keith Barker we find a *visual game of hide and seek* as the reader searches for a rainbow-striped snake who slithers through balls of wool, hats, cats, cakes, socks and baskets. The images spread over two pages and the text is *rhyming*. This is the first of the books I have mentioned which invites the reader to play a game with the images on the pages. Barker's books are well worth looking at.

In *Each, Peach, Pear, Plum* Janet and Allan Ahlberg play not only with rhyme but with *intertextuality*. In this wonderful book the children encounter characters and scenes from other books and nursery rhymes. Here is Tom Thumb, Mother Hubbard, Baby Bunting and more. But do be aware of just how culturally specific this is and take account of what it assumes about the prior experience of its readers. I'm not suggesting you don't read the book but do be aware that many of the children you work with may not know the nursery rhyme characters referred to. Share nursery rhymes and playground chants with them.

The makers of early picturebooks make narratives interesting and accessible to children as they begin to structure their own experience, which includes hearing stories read and told, to enable them to create their own narrative and re-tell stories they have heard. Many of these picturebooks seek to find ways of allowing the child to take over the role of reader from the adult. But there is more to picturebooks than being tools into independent reading. Good books speak to children in particular ways. They are about the issues that matter to children.

### The underlying meaning of picturebooks.
What is it about some picturebooks that make them so significant for individual children? Few children are really passionate about details like colour or shape or the names of days of the week or months of the year. Some may develop a passion for the patterns they find in numbers or the details of maps or the stars in the sky. There are some books that seem to speak to children, allowing them to explore safely some of the deep issues that preoccupy or concern them. Living in a world in which both good and bad things happen, children develop fears, worries and anxieties. They wonder why they don't love the new baby the way it seems they are supposed to. Or think about what might happen to them if mum dies or dad goes away. They can't come to

terms with having thrown a stone at the cat or scratched the child next to them. Living and dealing with their preoccupations and concerns as well as their passions and desires is important in their learning and development. Through fiction they can encounter such issues through the safety and anonymity of other imagined lives and worlds where they can deal with them without consequence.

Seven year old Maggie chose some 'best books ever' and, when asked why, she gave this wonderful personal and incisive response.

> I love *Not Now Bernard* and *Noisy Norah* because I often feel left out just like Bernard and just like Nora. Sometimes I want to throw things or leave home. I don't, in the end 'cos I know my mum loves me. And the new baby... and you know that book *Elmer*, well that is about how I sometimes feel when they tease me because I have got red hair. I think my hair is lovely but they call me nasty names and I don't like it. Elmer got teased too. I used to love best *Where the Wild Things Are* and that was because I often got cross and did naughty things and then was sent to my room – like Max. And those wild things. Wow! They were so scary. But in the end, you know, he just went back to his room. Maybe it was just a dream. I don't know. I like *Titch* now because I feel really sorry when all he gets are other peoples things. He just sometimes wants new things but because he is just a little kid like me, my mum says he is powerless. Kids like us don't have power, my mum says.' (Personal communication, 2010)

There are picturebooks that deal with death, fear of the dark, being abandoned, being lost, being new, having to change home or start school or go past a scary dog or have a birthday party or get into trouble or fail or be left out or lonely. These are serious human concerns that at times apply to us all and small children need to be able to explore these deep themes through the safety of picturebooks. If you have not yet encountered Michael Rosen's *Sad Book*, illustrated with spare line drawings by Quentin Blake, I suggest you do. Written after the death of his son Eddie, this book is a powerful and moving account of the impact of death. It is not, of course, written for very young children, but when my young grandson experienced the death of someone he loved he read and read and read this book. He was 10 years old at the time. He said 'It's the saddest book I ever read but it helps me. I don't know how'.

## Reading the text: reading the pictures

Anthony Browne's books have won numerous awards and they always deal with deep issues – which does not mean they are not funny, always inventive and revealing. Mostly he illustrates his own narratives and he says that in doing this he needs to make the pictures tell part of the story that the words don't. For me he is the supreme maker of books carrying multiple stories.

In writing his famous book *Gorilla* Browne was influenced by the film King Kong and thought about the gorilla as both a fierce creature in love with a young woman, as in the film, and as a macho gorilla yet needing and wanting the comfort of a teddy bear. The book is full of gorillas because the hero of the book, Hannah, is obsessed with them. They live in her head. She reads about them, watches programmes on television about them, draws them and is fascinated by them. On her birthday her father promises to give her a real gorilla but what he gives her is a toy gorilla, which she throws on the floor in disgust. And that is when something amazing happens – it is a story, after all! She meets this gorilla in the night. Is he her father? Is he real? Browne uses visual language to tell part of the story which he felt words alone could not tell. To highlight the different relationship Hannah has with her father to the one she has with the gorilla he drew two pictures. In the first Hannah and her father are seated at the breakfast table; in the second Hannah and the gorilla are having a meal in a cafe later that night. In the picture of home Browne adopts a perspective which exaggerates the the gap between them. The text just says 'Hannah's father didn't have time to take her to the zoo'. Browne says

> I used very geometric shapes – squares, triangles, hard edge, sharp angles – everything is neat and tidy, cold, clinical. I used blues, whites and greys – cold colours on everything apart from Hannah. Everything is smooth, hard – there is no real texture there' (1994:187)

In the picture of Hannah and the gorilla in the cafe the text says

> Hannah said 'I am hungry'.
> 'OK' said gorilla 'Let's eat.'

Here Browne has flattened the perspective to make the gorilla appear closer to the little girl. The intention is to make everything feel lifelike, touchable and tasty. To achieve this he used lots of texture and warm colours.

### Who is the implied reader?

Early picturebooks are written and illustrated for a presumed audience of young children. These young children grow up with visual images – some on walls in frames, on hoardings advertising things to buy, on television or screens of one kind or another. So though not all children have stories told or read to them almost all encounter visual images, and their knowledge of these images is both culture bound and taken for granted. Often those sharing picturebooks with young children spend time helping and encouraging them to read the text – to recognise words, name letters, memorise and join in with those repeated refrains. That the children will read the pictures is not always addressed. It is as though the adults reading to the children feel that the function of the images is solely to support how the child makes sense of the text. This is often true but as Anthony Browne reminds us the pictures often tell things that go beyond the text. And since the books are almost always read by adults to children, the adults become part of the implied readership. Let's not forget that adults read pictures in comics, graphic novels, on television, in film, in magazines. So a good maker of picturebooks or children's films thinks not only of the implied child but also of the accompanying adult. Think about films like *Shrek* or *Toy Story* where the sophisticated humour, references and subtle or not-so subtle subtexts appeal to the adults watching alongside the children.

John Burningham's books are wonderfully multilayered, offering readers the opportunity to explore one narrative from different perspectives. An ordinary event, like a day at the seaside, can become two completely different narratives, each seen from the perspective of one or another character. *'Come Away from the Water, Shirley'* tells just such a story of a family's day at the seaside but alongside, and in counterpoint, is Shirley's fantasy and her imagined encounter with pirates. This shows the young reader that stories can be changed; they can depend on who tells the story and how they tell it. It is a lesson they may already have encountered in their readings of wordless picturebooks.

Just as brilliant and possibly even more challenging is *Where's Julius?* about which Margaret Meek (1991:119) says that the pictures 'take their revenge on the text'. The Troutbeck family have three meals a day. When the meal is ready, a parent asks 'Where's Julius?' No response is given in the text; rather the artist takes over and Julius is seen doing things like digging a hole, building a house out of old curtains, chairs and a broom, throwing snowballs at Russian wolves and other fantastic activities. Meek says 'The narrative trick is: the story cannot be retold from an attempt to describe the pictures ... the events of Julius's imagination, are beyond words'(p120). Watching and listening to a child looking at this book is fascinating as the child not only makes sense of the parallel stories but gets drawn into simultaneous worlds.

It is also interesting to notice how differently a child and an adult make the narrative their own in these parallel texts. In *The Shape Game* by Anthony Browne (2003), created while he was writer and illustrator in residence at Tate Britain in London, he worked with a thousand children from inner city schools, teaching literacy using the resources of the gallery. At the end he produced this book – the story of mum, dad, George and his brother going to visit an art gallery. George and dad are missing an important football match and not really keen on looking at paintings. The idea of visiting an art gallery was mum's. Dad spent the day telling bad jokes and making negative comments about the works of art. On one page there is a picture called 'The Meeting or have a Nice Day, Mr Hockney' by Peter Blake. The text on the page repeats one of dad's bad jokes:

'Did you hear about the little boy they named after his father? asked dad.

'No' I said.

'They called him Dad!' said Dad.

There was a loud silence, but we all started laughing when we saw a painting of a man who looked a bit like Dad.

On the facing page there is a picture which is an enlarged adaptation of Blake's painting.

This is what happened when 4 year old Samuel was looking at the book with his father, Adam. Adam read the text and pointed to one feature of the painting on the facing page. It showed the main figure wearing dad's clothes and holding a huge fork with a sausage stuck on the prongs. Samuel would not let his dad turn the page to carry on until he had scrutinised the picture for a long time. At last he said:

'Hey dad, look at this. They are all dad. Even the dog has got dad's face. And the girl on roller skates is also dad. A girl is a man! (chuckles) And here is dad wearing a swimming costume and one of his roller skates looks like a fox's face. And that wall – in the first picture it's got words on. In this big one it's got pictures – a heart and pants and things. It's all the same and all different. There's lots more in this picture than in the words.' (Personal communication, 2011)

This seems to be a perfect illustration of Allan Ahlberg's words

The big truth about picturebooks ... is that they are an interweaving of word and picture. You don't have to tell the story in words. You can come out of the words and into the pictures and you get this nice kind of antiphonal fugue effect. (cited in Moss, 1990:21)

## Let me into this world

The world of children's literature has changed since 1965 when Nancy Larrick, author and anthologist of children's books, a teacher and critic, talked of 'The All-White World of Children's Books'. In Britain there were serious and significant attempts during the 1980s to address this issue with people like Judith Elkin (author of *Books for the Multi-Racial Classroom*), Rosemary Stones (author of *Don't Pick on Me*) and Gillian Klein (who is publishing this book and whom I met many years ago when she was librarian at the ILEA's Centre for Urban Educational Studies) writing or finding or commissioning or publishing books which reflect our multicultural world.

Verna Wilkins founded Tamarind Books in 1987 with the express purpose of redressing the balance in publishing by giving a high and positive profile to children from ethnic minorities. Tamarind Books has received recognition and rewards, most recently the Decibel Award for Cultural Diversity in 2008. The situation was so grave that teachers began to try and write their own books and draw parents into bookmaking workshops to try and produce materials more respectful and representative of this rich diversity.

It is shocking that in some ways things seem to have gone backwards. Go into any bookshop with a section for children, any library, look at any online book-seller and you will find many books with titles reflecting the smallness of our world. There are dozens of books with titles like *Shanyi Goes to China* or *Bongani's Day* or *J is for Jamaica*. Many offer stories illustrated with photographs. Some have exotic traditional tales told in English – and sometimes in English and another language. There is some celebration of difference but that does little to help a single black child in a Welsh village or an Iraqi child in Manchester identify with characters in picturebooks.

There is some awareness of the need for children to find themselves and their cultures and their experiences displayed in books. But it is difficult to find picturebooks doing the things that the books described above do – which is to offer possibilities for readings of both text and image, for exploring deep and difficult issues and for exploring things like humour and fantasy and co-incidence and plot. There are, of course, notable exceptions. You may know the books of Verna Aardema, *Why Mosquitoes Buzz* (with Dillon and Dillon), *Bringing the Rain to Kapiti Plain* (illustrated by Beatriz Vidal) and others, and the work of Eileen Browne in *Handa's Surprise* and *Handa's Hen* and David Mills and Derek Brazell's *Lima's Red Hot Chilli*. And you may have encountered some of the Mantra Lingua books like *Mei Ling's Hiccups*, or North South's selection which includes *My Mother's Sari*. Floella Benjamin wrote a book called *My Two Grannies* about a little girl with one grandmother from Yorkshire and the other from Trinidad. Illustrated by Margaret Chamberlain, it is gentle and affectionate but tends to gloss over issues and reflect two-dimensional characters.

A few picturebooks go further. There are two books by Nicola Campbell, both beautifully illustrated by Kim LaFave, one called *Shi-Shi-Etko* and the other *Shin-Chi's Canoe*. The author is Canadian and the books deal with the experiences of a girl and her brother who are sent off to a residential school and have to deal with important and universal issues like loneliness. Also wonderful is a book by Eve Bunting called *Smoky Night*, with dark and complex illustrations by David Diaz. The winner of the Caldecott Medal, it tells of the experience of a child, his family and their neighbours on a night of riots in Los Angeles.

Some artists and authors use fantastic creatures or animals instead of humans. These have human characteristics, family structures, social networks and feelings just like humans and by implication are almost culture-free, if that is possible. A master of this is Martin Waddell and if you are not familiar with his books you have a treat in store. *Owl Babies* is the story of three baby owls, Sarah and Percy and Bill who wake up in the night to find their mother gone. They sit and wait and wait, as it gets dark. Then they begin to worry about their mother. But of course she does comes back – and with food – and all ends well. The text is simple but threaded with rhythm and pace. The illustrations by Patrick Benson perfectly capture the anxiety, interdependence and eventual joy of the baby owls.

*Farmer Duck*, with illustrations by Helen Oxenbury, is a story of exploitation and group action. The farmer is lazy and stays in bed all day reading the newspaper and eating chocolates, whilst his poor duck has to do all the work on the farm. At last the poor duck collapses in tears, exhausted and has to be comforted by the chickens. They decide to take their revenge on the farmer, which they do. The text reads like a poem; the drawings are detailed and witty. The book has won many awards.

## The themes explored

In picturebooks there are two sets of symbols to explore – words and pictures. And as this chapter argues, sometimes each offers different stories. There are so many picturebooks currently available in print, not only as books to be read but also to be looked at as e-readers, or watched and heard as films or DVDs or cartoons or played as games, that the themes explored seem almost infinite. Certainly we find children's day to day concerns of feeling angry or jealous or left out or different or frightened explored across the genre. And we also find complex picturebooks which deal with war and becoming a refugee or witnessing fighting in the streets or feeling depressed. It is worth reiterating that the opportunity for children to deal with such difficult and troubling issues within the safety of narrative is very important.

## The child's work

Children can have a long and often passionate involvement with picture-books during the years they are becoming narrators and exploring all the complex and intricate relationships they have within their families, communities, settings and groups. Books create opportunities for them to find stories through both the pictures and the text, whether or not the illustrations tell parallel stories.

As budding readers, the children inevitably begin to pay attention to the marks on the page, and when they are sensitively supported in making sense of these marks, they learn that these are what makes the story the adult reads to them stay the same on each telling. How remarkable it must seem when the pictures can tell different stories each time they are looked at.

Sometimes the themes of the books speak clearly to individual children about their own concerns or interests, fears or feelings. I remember a little girl telling me that she loved *Dogger* better than any other book because she had lost her teddy and that had made her very sad.

Children learn that the fonts and the style of print can vary from page to page and can think about why this might happen. Why, for example, is the word 'Boo' written: BOO!? What do those dots on the page mean ... and why is there a bubble coming out of this character's mouth? Endless questions as they make sense of the narrative, and also of the book itself, of the text and the design.

Children are often drawn into the process of reading the text by the devices used by the writer – repetitive text, cumulative sentences, opportunities to join in and so on. Children are invited also to physically join in when they need to lift a flap or turn a page or are asked to go back to check what happened before.

## Building a culture and pedagogy based on narrative

■ Read to children individually, in pairs, in small groups, in larger groups, often and every day. Some books are better read to individual children; some to small groups. Use enlarged texts and formats when reading to larger groups to draw the children more easily into the details of the pictures and the features of text.

■ Leave the books you have read out so the children can re-tell the stories for themselves using text and image. Sometimes include small world figures or cut-outs of the characters in the story alongside the book to help children with little or no English re-create the story or make up another.

■ Allow children time to examine the pictures. This should be encouraged and seen as part of the process of making meaning and hence part of the process of reading. The child is attempting to lift the meaning – all of it – from the pages.

■ Be selective in what books you make available. Just as with wordless books, think about the deeper themes and issues explored in the books, the quality of the language used and the images offered, the relevance for the children, the opportunities to allow them to use their prior experience to relate to the narrative.

■ Ask yourself questions about what your little library offers to girls and boys, children new to the country, children speaking languages other than English, urban children and rural children. If you find, as you almost invariably will, gaps in your provision go to your local library (if it still exists) or to a good children's bookshop or to the children's section of a good bookshop and browse.

# 6

## The tale visualised in your head

I told her that I was in the first grade already,
strong like her and all grown up
and then I dried the tears from her eyes,
opened my arms and let my mommy go.
(From *I Helped My Mom Not to Be Late for Work* by Carmen Lucca)

In this chapter we move on from books with both words and pictures telling the story or stories to books where there are no pictures that carry the story. Young children call them 'chapter books' and see reading them as a significant step in growing up.

### The power and the passion

When even very young children are interested in and passionate about something they can pay attention for a long time, contrary to what the media would have us believe. When an adaptation of Phillip Pullman's series *His Dark Materials* was being produced at the National Theatre I took Hannah to see the first of the two three-hour long plays. She sat there totally engrossed and involved and at the end of the performance she pleaded with me to book for the second performance. She was quite clear that she didn't want to go home and come back at a later date. She had to see the work through to the end. And stay we did. She was only 7 at the time.

This illustrates just how powerful a story can be when a child like Hannah has listened to it from beginning to end in a non-stressful, non-questioning, non-judgmental environment. The readings of the books were part of the normal day and both Hannah and her mother enjoyed them. Pullman's series is complex and full of ideas, arguments, dilemmas and problems. They are a mixture of the real and the fantastic. There were certainly many things in that story that

Hannah did not fully understand but there was enough in there to engage her interest, allow her to make worlds in her head, links with her own experience and engagement with the characters.

Hannah later read the books for herself and told me that features of the play had accorded with her impressions of the characters and events and delighted her. Others did not and this sometimes vexed her. When she went to see the American film version, *The Golden Compass*, she hated it because little fitted with the personal meanings she had made about the characters and themes of the original and because the ending had been changed. Hannah had had the good fortune to have heard the books read, read them herself, seen the plays and the film. What all that enabled her to do was to become critical, comparing one version with another and deciding what most spoke to her. Becoming able to make a comparison and a judgment is a crucial cognitive skill which all children need to develop. Hannah is an advantaged child, but there is no reason that all children should not have access to at least some of the things Hannah had.

The *2011 Dimbleby Lecture* was given by Michael Morpurgo. His theme was the rights of children and he spoke passionately about what he believed all children should be entitled to and, as a writer and storyteller, he told stories to illustrate his points forcefully. He ended his talk by considering what happens to human infants, each born as what he called a 'unique genius', many doomed to grow up with a fear of failure, much of which he attributed to our education system and our schools and settings. He stated that we are so busy measuring minor aspects of learning and development that we ignore the most important things that children learn – about relationships, themselves, other people and feelings. Like the wonderful educators in the famed nursery schools in Reggio Emilia, Morpurgo wants to see what they call 'a pedagogy of relationships'. He asks all teachers and other educators, particularly those involved with young children, to spend, at a minimum, the last half hour of each day reading to the children, with no tests, no questions, just the pleasure, the power and the passion of the children, the adult and the story.

## The cognitive and emotional challenges

Young children make meaning from all that happens to them. From this they begin to sequence key events in their daily lives into narratives as they reflect on what happened, in what order, what mattered and why. Making everyday narratives seems simple to us but for young children it is an intricate and challenging intellectual task.

Two year old Sacha's little narrative goes like this 'I dropped the cup. It went on the floor. My mum was cross. She shouted'.

What has Sacha had to know and do to make this narrative? She has to know that dropping the cup had consequences which made her mother angry. Her mother's anger was scary. One way of dealing with unpleasant feelings is to share them.

Children become storytellers partly because they hear people telling stories about everyday events, partly through stories watched, heard or read. Stories read and told offer models of more complex and varied ways of selecting events, sequencing them, structuring them into a conventional format with a beginning, middle and end.

The cognitive and emotional challenges include the following:

- As children begin to tell stories they become part of communities of story-makers, sharing with them ways of making and telling stories.

- Using *book language*, which is different from everyday language, and inviting the use of *comparison, simile, metaphor, repetition, rhyme, rhythm* and more.

- Reflecting on what they have heard and remembered to help them think about or predict what happens next. The roles of *memory* and *prediction* are important in learning and, combined with *reflection,* help children become critical and thinking readers.

- Appreciating how a story can be about something real or imaged and fantastic. This helps them understand the differences between real and possible, tangible and imagined. They can explore the power of using fantasy in dealing with difficult issues not only in their narratives but in their lives.

- Seeing the *boundary between the real and the possible,* the actual and the potential is a powerful emotional tool.

- Making their own images from the words they hear, in the absence of images. This allows them to develop worlds in their heads. They learn about different times and places, various ways of living now and then and in the future; relationships, styles of interacting and family structures. So they learn about wonder of diversity.

- Becoming able to see the characters, places, era, events in ways related to their own experience and culture. Each story they hear allows them to develop a greater sense of the possible range of of these. The more stories they hear and read the wider their experience becomes.

■ Knowing that a story can be read or interpreted in a number of ways so that a simple story can be a *metaphor for something else.* This helps them decode many of the messages that they receive which are often veiled, coded or hinted at.

■ Learning not only about the deep and difficult issues that affect them and their feelings but how to deal with them. They listen to how others have encountered and dealt with things like anger, loneliness, loss, fear, jealousy, envy, losing a parent or a home or adapting to somewhere or something new. The stories they hear help them in the narratives they make which allow them to express their fears and feelings and share them. These are vital steps in the process of reaching emotional independence and maturity.

In effect children use the stories they hear to make sense of what Bruner so brilliantly called the 'actual and the possible worlds'. Those who have access to stories in all their forms and formats can draw on a wide range of influences in their own story-making and thinking.

## The features of story books with few or no illustrations
*Increased complexity of plot; use of time and space and character*
In an extended story, going from a beginning through many events, there may be twists and turns, problems encountered and overcome, changes over time, mood and place. This allows children to create whole worlds peopled by a range of characters rich and poor, young and old, powerful and feeble, real and fantastic, ordinary or magical.

The picturebooks encountered earlier generally dealt with a much smaller range of events and narrower time frame.

Let's take a fairly simple chapter book as a starting point for analysis.

*Flat Stanley*, written by Jeff Brown and illustrated by Tomi Ungerer, is the story of a perfectly ordinary boy who wakes up one morning completely flat. His parents have to peel an incriminating bulletin board off him, after which he begins to live in his new form. He finds he can slide under doors, fish his mother's ring out of a narrow metal grating, fit into an envelope to be posted and so on. There is a fine adventure when he stops a gang of thieves from stealing paintings from the Famous Museum of Art. It all ends happily, of course, through the intervention of his brother.

The pictures illustrate the story rather than telling a different or parallel story. It is up to the listener to make the 'pictures'. *Flat Stanley* is similar to a picture-book but there is more than one event or journey in it and this leads the listener to begin to think about what might happen next. Prediction, an important cognitive skill, is essential to becoming a narrator.

### The use of memory, inference and prediction in making meaning

Both prediction and memory play a role in making sense of any story, be it told in picture, words or both. In a longer story, however, more happens; there are often a host of characters and it is important for the listener to remember who is who, what their relationship is to other characters, what has already happened and why. The listener needs to know these things in order to make sense of the story.

Here is an example of what happened to Rashida, who had missed some of what had already been read. Beverley Naidoo's *Journey to Joburg* is a story set in apartheid South Africa. Three children, 13 year old Naledi, her younger brother Tiro and their baby sister, are black and poor. Their mother has had to leave them in the care of their grandmother in the countryside to get work which she can only find in the city. When the baby falls ill the children decide to go and find their mother. On the journey they encounter and suffer the consequences of apartheid. One of the children in the class, Rashida, was absent for the first two weeks the book was being read in assembly in a London school. So she had missed the introductory talk and the first two chapters. She knew nothing about apartheid, with its racist denial of basic human rights for the majority black population. For her the story started a good way through and although she soon remembered who each of the key characters was and could work out why they were going on the journey, she found it almost impossible to pick up on the inferences about being black during apartheid. She could only draw partially on memory because her memory started some way into the story. She was lucky in that the pull of the journey kept her engaged with predicting whether or not the children would find their mother and bring her home to the baby.

### The role of inference in literature

Authors often use the device of suggesting or inferring rather than simply stating. Louis Sacher's popular book *Holes* tells how Stanley Yelnats got into trouble and was offered a choice of sentence by the judge. He could either go to jail or to Camp Green Lake. He was from a poor family and had never been to camp before. See how this description of what happened one day at breakfast enables you to work out what sort of place Stanley had landed in.

Stanley was half asleep as he got in line for breakfast, but the sight of Mr. Sir awakened him. The left side of Mr. Sir's face had swollen to the size of half a cantaloupe. There were three dark-purple jagged lines running down his cheek where the Warden had scratched him.

The other boys in Stanley's tent had obviously seen Mr. Sir as well, but they had the good sense not to say anything. Stanley put a carton of juice and a plastic spoon on his tray. He kept his eyes down and hardly breathed as Mr. Sir ladled some oatmeal-like stuff into his bowl.

He brought his tray to the table. Behind him, a boy from one of the other tents said, 'Hey, what happened to your face?'

There was a crash.

Stanley turned to see Mr. Sir holding the boy's head against the oatmeal pot. 'Is something wrong with my face!'

The boy tried to speak but couldn't. Mr. Sir had him by the throat.

'Does anyone see anything wrong with my face?' asked Mr. Sir, as he continued to choke the boy.

Nobody said anything.

Mr. Sir let the boy go. His head banged against the table as he fell to the ground.

Mr. Sir stood over him and asked, 'How does my face look to you now?'

A gurgling sound came out of the boy's mouth, then he managed to gasp the word, 'Fine.'

'I'm kind of handsome, don't you think?'

'Yes, Mr. Sir.'

By not saying anything directly, but inferring it, the author gives the reader a vivid sense of what the place was like. You get a clear feeling about the embedded brutality of the place.

*Authors use figurative language involving devices like simile and metaphor as a way of helping readers compare the unfamiliar with the everyday*

A whole theme in a book stands for or represents something else – the classic example is C.S.Lewis's *The Lion, the Witch and the Wardrobe*. On the surface this is a story about four children evacuated during the war to a dark house in the country, where one child finds and enters a wardrobe which then gives access to the mysterious and complex land of Narnia. The children have adventures with strange creatures and encounter Aslan, the Lion, who dies and is later resurrected, the Witch and others. I read the book to 7 year olds over a period of time, not recognising that the whole book is a metaphor for Christianity. We read it as an adventure story. When Aslan died many of the children began to cry. Literature has this power to allow and enable children to express such feelings of loss and grief.

## Of love and loss and tragedy and hope and friendship and more

When I was compiling this section I asked some young people to think of the stories they had heard read in primary school which made a deep impression on them. All of them chose stories dealing with serious and deep issues.

Lucy remembered *The Thief Lord*, written by Cornelia Funke, which she said 'is a kind of detective story set in Venice. The cast of characters includes 12 year old Prospero and his 5 year old brother Bo, recently orphaned and fleeing home because an aunt offered to adopt Bo but not his older brother.' The themes Lucy identified in this book included the loss and potential loss of friendships and trust; unfairness and how hard but exciting it is to begin a new life in a strange place. Lucy loved the idea of the city of Venice and the fact that the boys had chosen it because their mother had talked to them about it. She loved the sense of darkness and light of the city which are reflected in the twisting turns of the story.

Joti chose Eva Ibbotson's *Journey to the River Sea* which is about Maia, a little orphaned girl, who is sent from her home in England to live with relatives on their rubber plantation on the banks of the Amazon River – another story about a child having to adapt to life in a new and strange place. Joti said he particularly liked the rich cast of characters including a travelling actor who misses home in England, a rich Finnish heir who wants not to return to England and two other orphans. Joti loved the many adventures the characters had in search of a legendary giant sloth.

Jacob loved *Granny Torrelli Makes Soup* by Sharon Creech. This is about 12 year old Rosie and her best friend, visually impaired Bailey, who have fallen out because Rosie has started to learn Braille. Jacob said 'I think that knowing Braille is something that Bailey can do and because he is the only one who can do it he feels special about it. He resents Rosie for trying to take this away from him. Or that's how he sees it.' The problem is resolved as Granny Torrelli cooks, shares her recipes and her stories in the warm and fragrant kitchen. This is a story about daily life, and the importance of culture and relationships. It is about friendship and family and is a story full of stories. As Jacob put it 'It's like one of those Russian dolls only it's not dolls inside one another, it's stories'.

Fatih, himself once a refugee, recommended Benjamin Zephaniah's book *Refugee Boy*. Zephaniah is a poet with a strong political thread running through his poems and stories. *Refugee Boy* may be a book for children to grow into but it may be of particular relevance to children who are refugees. It is the story of 14 year old Alem, brought to England ostensibly on holiday, but then abandoned with only a letter of explanation. His parents are, in fact, fighting for the emancipation of their people in Ethiopia and Eritrea. Alem has to find a way of being given political asylum in the UK. The young boy experiences deep emotions, particularly when he hears that his mother has died but he forms strong relationships in his new home and culture. Fatih said 'It was difficult to follow sometimes, but for me it was really perfect. It talked of so many of the things that had happened to me and to my family. It brought back horrible memories but because we were listening to it as a group it somehow made me feel less separate, more one of the group'. The experience allowed Fatih and the other children to become part of a community of listeners to narrative.

Rahel selected Michael Morpurgo's *The Kites are Flying*. Rahel said that she loved listening to this story because she has a friend who doesn't ever talk and the book helped her understand why. She said 'It is about Max, a journalist who travels to the West Bank to see what it is like to live under the shadow of the giant wall they have built. Then he makes friends with a Palestinian boy called Said and Said shows Max how he makes kites. Said does not talk. Then Max finds out the terrible things that happened to Said and understands why he doesn't talk now'. This is a story of tragedy, of friendship and the building of trust, and of hope.

### The themes explored

There are as many themes involved in longer books or films as in the wordless and picturebooks written expressly for younger children. What these longer books are able to do, however, is to explore the themes in more detail and depth and perhaps move away from the standard format of the happy ending. Some skilled authors, like Phillip Pullman, create an open-ended ending which can be interpreted as either happy or not. As children get older they become more and more aware of the realities of life and the issues facing people on a daily basis and they begin to realise that real life involves things which are not always happily resolved.

Hannah at the age of 4 said 'All stories with a happy ending have a bad character in them'. Then she paused to think and continued 'except for *The Secret Garden*'. A complex analysis of stories watched on film, heard in books or told had allowed her to reach this conclusion. She had to work out what good and bad means in terms of characters, understand that stories include made up people who are called characters and come to terms with the feature of many stories which is that only when something bad has been overcome can there be a happy ending. Quite a cognitive feat – yet most of our very young children can do this.

## The child's work

What the child has to do when listening to a longer story is to listen, get involved, remember events and characters and come to realise that personal gratification is delayed. The story will go on over a long period of time with gaps during which the child can think back on what has already happened and guess at what might happen next. Experiencing suspense in this way is unlikely to be unfamiliar to our children, reared as they are on soap operas with their ongoing sagas, episode after episode. But it is different from listening to a story told in entirety in one sitting or looking at a picturebook alone or with an adult. So the child has to develop the cognitive skills of being able to think about something that is not present, visually, physically, or aurally, and retain that.

The child also needs to make sense of some of the devices authors introduce into stories. Skilled authors often say things indirectly, just as skilled artists imply rather than make obvious. The reader or beholder must do the work of sorting out the meaning. Consider which of these ways of telling is more interesting: 'I walked into the room and there, on the floor was a streak of blood. The door of the birdcage was open and the bird was not longer there. And on the floor the fat cat was purring happily' or 'The cat killed the bird'. In the first one the author has not actually told the reader that the cat ate the bird; the meaning has to be inferred. In *When Hitler Stole Pink Rabbit* by Judith Kerr, 9 year old Anna is growing up in Berlin in 1933. In the first chapter Kerr introduces the characters, who are primarily members of Anna's family, her friends and the servants. She also introduces a feeling of the growing atmosphere of fear at that time. At the end of the chapter Anna goes in to kiss her father goodnight and finds that he has gone. Chapter Two starts like this:

> Anna's first thought was so terrible that she could not breathe. Papa had got worse in the night. He had been taken to hospital.

This illustrates both the use of an ending which leaves the reader or listener wanting to know what will happen next and hinting at rather than stating. The reader must predict, based on what has been read and experienced or known before. If you have read the book or know about the fate of most of Berlin's Jews, you will know that what follows will be bleak.

## Building a culture and pedagogy based on narrative

- Become acquainted with chapter books and consider which might be relevant to the interests of the children in the group. This requires time but it will be time well and pleasurably spent. Seek the advice of the children in your group, go to the local library, browse in the children's section of any good bookshop, ask your friends and colleagues and draw on your own favourites. And, importantly, have high expectations of the children. You will be amazed at how involved they can become in longer stories and how much they will think about the issues raised.

- Try and develop your skill at pacing the reading so that you end leaving the listeners wanting more.

- At the beginning of each session find ways of recapping what has happened by reminding the children directly or inviting a child whose memory you know you can rely on to tell any child who was absent at the previous session what has happened.

- When you encounter something you think might require explanation because the children cannot have any possibility of understanding through lack of experience, offer an explanation and invite the children to ask questions at the end of the session.

- Try and build a culture of listening. Our society is one of almost constant sound or noise and many children find it difficult to remain quiet. There is something really magical in helping children cohere as a silent group, all gripped by the power of the story. One way of helping achieve this is by taking children to the theatre, where a culture of listening exists.

# 7
## Who's culture is it?

Many grandmothers like to bake cookies and cakes,
*mi abuela* likes to make *tortillas y empanadas*.
Some grandmothers enjoy reading and sewing,
*mi abuela* enjoys softball and my swings.
(From *Mi abuela* by Cristina Muniz Mutchler)

Recently I was invited to watch a film clip on youtube and when I heard that it featured the winner of Ukraine's Got Talent I felt myself bristle. All my prejudices about what I categorised as high or low culture came into play but I watched it and was astounded. A young Ukrainian woman, Kseniya Simonova, was telling the story of the Second World War using a light tray, sand and her amazingly skilled hands and fingers. It is worth trying to watch this to see this consummate storyteller and artist, conveying an enormous amount of information and feeling purely through images. My initial response mirrors that of educators who make judgements about certain things that most please young children – the things they do out of school, out of the classroom, rarely alone, sometimes with family members, often in the streets and usually with peers. What binds them to one another through what is shared is what we label as popular culture.

## Popular culture
We tend to differentiate in this society between popular culture and high culture. Put baldly literature and opera and theatre are seen as high culture and the preserve of the educated and cultured in society. Popular culture, what is seen on television, shared online, listened to by the young, read in magazines and comics, is seen as less demanding, less important, and less valuable. It is even perceived as dangerous. We make easy value judgements, often without

knowing enough about just what it is that draws people to what they watch and read and listen to.

A few years ago a South African theatre group took Mozart's famous opera, *The Magic Flute* and transformed it into an African version, *Impempe Yomlingo*. Instead of a symphony orchestra playing the sublime music, it was all played on traditional marimbas supported by drums. Some people loved it; many hated it and regarded it as a travesty. In a similar boundary-crossing exercise the National Theatre recently offered a sell-out and brilliant production by film director Danny Boyle of Mary Shelley's *Frankenstein*. High culture, popular culture, neither or both? These terms are not very helpful but what is clear is that we, as people involved with young children, should not ignore what interests and fascinates them.

## Overheard in the playground

The narratives children share with their peers are primarily but not solely based on the narratives they find on television, computer screens and other media. If you eavesdrop on children in the playground or lunch room you will hear them earnestly discussing events in soap operas, comparing the exploits of various superheroes, and suggesting strategies for playing the games on their electronic gadgets.

Young children are immersed in practices relating to popular culture, media and new technologies from birth. Our world is a digital world and young children need to develop a wide range of skills, knowledge and understanding to understand, explain, describe, participate in and share it. Children learn to make sense of the digital world largely in their homes at first, where their parents and family scaffold their learning. This scaffolding may be done implicitly or explicitly, as children engage in family social and cultural practices which develop their understanding of the role of media and technology in society.

In a study called *Digital beginnings: Young children's use of popular culture, media and new technologies* (2005) a surprisingly positive picture emerged of the role of popular culture in the lives of young children. Jackie Marsh and her fellow researchers interviewed nearly 2000 parents and carers of children who attended 120 early years settings in England, maintained and non-maintained. The parents told them that their young children generally led 'well-balanced lives' where popular culture, media and new technologies played an important but not overwhelming role, in their leisure activities. The parents felt that the engagement of their children with media involved children in actively making meaning which extended into their play and their speaking and listening and narration of stories. They said the children's engagement with media and new technologies was done not on a solitary basis but in a social way, often alongside peers, siblings, family or community (Marsh *et al*, 2005).

But how about the educators of the children? Do they welcome and promote popular culture in their schools and settings? In the same study well over 500 practitioners were interviewed and they too expressed generally positive attitudes to the roles played by new technologies and media in the lives of the children, although some showed concern about the amount of time children spend in front of screens.

A year before this study Millard (2004) carried out a small piece of research interviewing six classroom teachers about their views on the use of popular culture in the literacy curriculum and although our focus is on literature rather than on literacy, the findings are relevant and interesting. Marsh focused primarily on the parents of younger children. She asked them about the literacy practices of their children – what their experiences of reading and writing out of school were – particularly those related to *technoliteracy*. One of the key areas she was interested in was multimodal literacy events which may be mediated by new technologies.

Parents were asked to keep diaries over four weeks, noting the titles and details of any texts with which their children engaged. Texts could be narratives on television, film, computer games or mobile phones. Her findings indicated that children engaged primarily with televisual texts but also with computer games, comics, books based on television characters, print in the environment linked to media, and texts on stickers and labels. Parents were supportive of how children used all texts as opportunities for making narratives and for play, and noted that the children often used the characters from televisual watching as potential roles in play, just as Hannah had played out episodes from the televisual experience of *The Secret Garden* with her plastic dinosaurs.

When parents were asked about their children's interest in computer games they said that many enjoyed PlayStation games. Half of the 4 year old children who did so were girls. However a marked gender difference emerged in older children: boys predominated and the researchers believed this was because boys were probably inducted into these games by the men of the family.

So children are deeply engaged with narratives in a range of forms and formats in their lives out of school. They enjoy a shared culture of the media.

If we are to draw children into the worlds of literature in its broadest sense we have to recognise these interests and passions and find ways of including them in the school or nursery setting.

## Unpopular culture?

There are both well-known and unsung practitioners who promote the recognition of popular culture in classrooms. In America in the 1990s Ann Haas Dyson, working with older children, noticed their absorption in the fantasy worlds of superheroes. She analysed how they became narrators as they imagined and re-imagined possible roles each might take and the words they might speak in these roles. She said that what this gave them was an ever-expanding world. And that is, of course, what literature, in all its guises, can do. Her book *Writing Superheroes: Contemporary Childhood, Popular Culture and Classroom Literacy* is well worth reading.

Also in America, working with the youngest children is Vivian Gussin Paley. Early in her career as kindergarten teacher, she recognised how important the making, acting and telling of narratives was in the lives of the young children in her care. Gradually she changed her way of teaching to hand control to the children and allow the setting to become an ever-changing open theatre where children could live their stories. Their stories could be about anything and everything that worried, excited or moved them. Do read Paley's books. They are full of enchanting, tragic, funny and moving children's narratives.

Despite such persuasive evidence about the importance of accepting popular culture into schools and settings, there are some places where this is not accepted. In a dated piece of research Julie Wollman-Bonilla looked at the perceptions of trainee and serving teachers at Rhode Island College in Providence, USA asking them to state which books, if any, would be unsuitable for use in classrooms. Wollman-Bonilla chose some of the books student teachers consistently rejected to read aloud and then asked the students to discuss their feelings about them. Their selection included some books I have mentioned: *Amazing Grace* which deals with overcoming both sexism and racism, *Smoky Night*, which deals with urban violence, prejudice and racism and *The Paper Bag Princess*, which challenges gender stereotyping.

Here are reasons they gave for why these books were thought to be inappropriate for children.

■ Books like this might frighten or corrupt children by introducing them to things they don't or should not know. *Bridge to Terabithia* was said to be too sad because it made children think about death. Comments about

*Smoky Night* included 'I don't think they need to think about riots' and 'Riots aren't part of their experience' (Wollman-Bonilla, 1998:289). Tell that to the children of Tottenham, Croydon, Hackney, Birmingham and Manchester.

▪ Books like this fail to represent the dominant social and cultural values, beliefs, myths and ideas. *The Paper-Bag Princess, Amazing Grace* and *William's Doll*, all of which challenge racism, sexism or both, were rejected on the grounds of 'modelling inappropriate English' or 'reinforcing stereotypes by being about a broken family where the grandmother speaks nonstandard English' (p290).

▪ Books like this identify issues like prejudice, racism, sexism as social problems. This is possibly the most interesting category because the responses of the trainee teachers are so revealing. In response to *The Paper Bag Princess* a male teacher said it was a terrible story with a 'lady' who is rude and aggressive. He added that he would not like girls to see this as acceptable behaviour. With regard to *William's Doll* teachers of both genders felt that a book showing boys playing with dolls could create controversy about appropriate ways for boys and girls to behave. And in regard to a book about racism one of the teachers felt anxious about using books which imply that black students might be offended by images which portrayed them as different, saying 'we should treat all the students the same'.

This research took place over a decade ago and some attitudes have, happily, changed, but there is still concern about using texts that reveal what critics call the darker side of life yet reflect the experience of many of today's children who still experience poverty, prejudice, racism, sexism, riots, discrimination, war, homelessness, loneliness and alienation.

## Cultural capital

One of the most vexing questions is why some groups of children are consistently less successful in our schooling system. Poverty certainly plays a pivotal role, as do factors like discrimination, prejudice, equity or lack of it. Today we still hear people talking about how some types of homes and families are 'better' than others at preparing children for success in schooling. It is rare to think about it from the opposite perspective – namely that some schools are better at enabling all children to succeed in learning.

Someone whose work has been important in this domain is Pierre Bourdieu, a French Marxist sociologist, who examined aspects of society in terms of power and class. Karl Marx believed that capital was power which is acquired through work or labour. If you work hard and earn a salary, that is your power. You can use it to acquire more capital in terms of a place to live, possessions and so on. Bourdieu (1977) believed the capital should also have a symbolic value that goes beyond the economic What he meant by symbolic was cultural, linguistic and social factors that can either help or hinder progress. We often hear it said that children who have English as an additional language, a single parent, parents who don't read to them or live in a deprived area are less likely to succeed in school. Cultural capital is what we have learned and know. You may have a PhD from one of the so-called Russell universities in the UK and thus hold a great deal of cultural capital. Or you may have no formal qualifications but have extensive work and life experience. You may well have as much cultural capital in terms of doing your job but less in the eyes of society. Linked to cultural capital is social capital which can be defined as who we know. It does not take much reflection to recognise how important this can be in situations where personal contacts open doors.

Bourdieu also talked of *habitus* which is a system of dispositions or attitudes that explain the differences we see in societies between and within groups. Children with a disposition to enjoy formal learning are more likely to succeed at school. Those with a disposition or habitus to enjoy books are more likely to become readers and love reading.

Children live in complex cultural worlds and they bring to each one a store of cultural capital. Where the cultural capital children bring to the classroom or setting is similar to and valued by that of the school or setting, the children are most likely to thrive. Where children bring cultural capital that is different from that of their educators, the educators may not know what to recognise and hence value. Bourdieu's ideas offer us tools to consider success and failure in terms of social and cultural capital. We can turn the spotlight on the school or setting rather than on the children and their families.

Prout (2005) said Bourdieu's analysis did not take full account of the fact that children are always active agents in their meaning making and in their acquisition of social capital. What children do is bring their own cultural and social capital and habitus to new situations and then appropriate and transform the cultures they encounter.

When Hannah first started school the cultural capital she brought included an intimate knowledge of stories in books and from videos. One of the ways in which she worked to use this cultural capital to become part of the new culture of school was to 'play' the stories that she knew in the school playground. This seemingly simple act requires an extremely complex exploration of cultural meanings. In a group, children, each with a unique habitus, must reach some agreement so they can inhabit a shared imaginary world. Each child has to have an identity and a place within the story, which they come to through exploring their own understandings, many of which will be drawn from their personal exposure to culture – popular and other. In doing this Hannah became, briefly, a cultural leader. In many other situations she was a cultural follower.

Paley (1988) shows how four year olds negotiate the roles they will play.

> 'Am I in your story?' Millie asks.
>
> 'Who do you want to be? The witch?'
>
> 'No I'll be Superwoman.'
>
> 'Oh. She didn't come in my story yet. I'll tell the teacher. Do you want Superwoman to kill the witch, Mollie?'
>
> Mollie considers the possibilities. 'Can I be the one who holds baby Superman?'
>
> 'Sure. Hey, guess what, Mollie! Pretend I'm the Superman dad and you're the Superwoman mom and we make the baby a little house, okay?'
>
> 'And a tiny tiny tiny bed' Mollie hums.
>
> 'For his tiny tiny tiny head' (p116-7)

The children express their preferences, draw on popular culture, listen to one another, try to accommodate each other's preferences and negotiate a mutually agreeable solution. What complex work this is – socially, intellectually and linguistically.

## Whose popular culture?

We talk of popular culture as though it is one thing. There are aspects of it that are mainstream – like Eastenders or Playstation games – but many minority cultures in the UK and elsewhere enjoy popular culture which comes about through and is transformed by global communication.

Kenner (2003) cites examples from a South London nursery project: 3 year old Billy's family are Thai and his favourite text in Thai was a karaoke video. Love songs were sung and acted out against a background of boats on a river, with the text of the words of the song rippling across the screen; Meera was in love with Bollywood films and in her favourites there were heroines dressed in black leather, challenging the dominance of male gangs.

Popular culture is not static but dynamic and is not the property of any one group. So in our schools and settings we need to be alert to the following:

- what children say and do in terms of mainstream and other popular culture

- children telling us and using aspects of what matters to them out of school in their in-school or setting experiences

- remaining largely non-judgmental about what children bring with them. We cannot afford to occupy some mythical high ground

- introducing some of 'our' culture to the children as something new, exciting, different and challenging

- enabling bilingual children to retain their languages and cultures partially through engaging with multilingual popular culture in their classrooms and settings.

## A word of warning

There are, however, aspects of popular culture which are cause for concern. On television, in adverts and in the clothes on sale for them, very young children are presented with over-sexualised images of what it means to be female. In the year 2011 pink was still seen as the colour expressing femininity. Boys continue to be offered images of strength and violence and physical power. Both genders find implications for their own sense of identity in terms of gender roles and what is regarded as acceptable in these images. Those who come from different cultures, speak languages other than English and have customs, beliefs and practices that are not those of the mainstream may also find themselves reflected in ways in which their experience is demeaned or ignored.

Henry Giroux, a distinguished professor at Penn State University, expresses great concern about the effect of the Disney phenomenon on children's thinking, meaning making and narration. Before the birth of his own children he had viewed the impact of animated films on children rather benignly, seeing them as stimulating the imagination through what was described as 'naive innocence and wholesome adventure'. But watching his own children and listening to what they said and did after watching these films began to make him uncomfortable about the values and attitudes they seemed to be promoting. He noted the profound influence of Disney as a producer of children's culture, and believed that this was reason for his work to be open to scrutiny and criticism. Disney certainly created colourful and enchanting worlds and in most of his films he explored the traditional features of children's narratives – the battles between good and evil, beautiful and ugly, old and young, rich and poor, powerful and powerless. These worlds have been portrayed in different ways by Hans Christian Anderson or the Brothers Grimm or J. M. Barrie or J.R.R.Tolkien or a host of others, using words and sometimes pictures.

Disney's celluloid worlds leave little to the imagination: everything is up there, larger than life, two-dimensional in every sense and using devices to represent or symbolise essential features – good and bad, old and young and so on. The good are almost invariably handsome, young, white, Anglo-Saxon whilst the bad might wield weapons, have gross facial features such as bulbous noses or speak with heavy accents of one sort or another.

Perhaps one of the most the most controversial examples of racist stereotyping occurs in his film *Aladdin* made in 1989. In the original version the words of the opening song went like this: 'Oh, I come from a land, from a faraway place – where the caravan camels roam. Where they cut off your ears if they don't like your face. It's barbaric, but hey, it's home'. Under pressure from outside these words were later changed. The hero, Aladdin, does not have a beard or a big nose or a turban and he doesn't have an accent: that is because he is 'the goodie'. How else would you recognise that? Facial features, styles of dress, ways of speaking become a shorthand – a semiotic system for helping children 'read' the meaning.

There are other examples of both sexism and racism in the films and Giroux argues that children learn through these films that 'different from' white American means 'deviant, inferior, stupid and dangerous'. Disney's influence shapes the 'symbolic environment into which our children are born and in which we all live our lives'. He argues not for censorship but for the need for children to be critical of what they encounter.

## Children's play and narrative in the new media age

It is reassuring to note that the most recent study on how the new media impact on children's play and story making has revealed that what children do is to use all their experience of new media as material for the games, rituals, stories, and scenarios they play at home, in parks, in the streets and in the playground and classroom or setting (Marsh *et al*, 2011). It is a very positive view of how children make and change culture in the digital age.

The British Library has set up a website at www.bl.uk/playtimes. It features experts and researchers including Andrew Burn and Steve Roud talking about the changing face of childhood over the last few decades; Rebekah Willet on how children bring imaginative narratives and language into all their play; Steve Roud, drawing on the research of Kathryn Marsh, on how children's games and songs have changed as communities become more diverse and also on the ways in which boys and girls play together in the playground; Chris Richards on the role of 'play fighting', suggesting children are aware that what they are doing is fantasy and pretense rather than reality; and Andrew Burn on the relationship between media cultures and 'traditional' play-ground games.

## The child's work

As always the work of the child is to make sense of what she is involved with. This is first done not in the formal setting of school but at home or in the community where the child is among more expert others who help induct her into making and sharing the meaning. When the child brings this culture to the classroom or setting she is the expert and is in the position to induct others into it. Kenner (2003) gives us the example of 5 year old Recep at a South London school who became an expert in a research project. The staff invited parents and relatives to bring newspapers in different languages to help children make their own newspapers. Recep recognised events and personalities in the Turkish newspaper brought in by his mother. He cut out pictures of his favourite singer Hulya Avsar and sang some of the songs he had heard her sing on TV. He talked knowledgeably about Turkish football teams. He recognised and named a photograph of Kemal Ataturk. Kenner's analysis of this was that the Turkish newspapers represented the cultural life of Recep's community and had strong emotional importance for him. He wrote with pride in Turkish, having never shown any interest in writing in English. Clearly children with more than one culture can experience both cultures as simultaneous and not as two separate worlds.

Children need to be able to interpret and use a range of semiotic systems. This implies using a range of consoles and remote controls, keyboards, and screens, large and small. There are other important and often transferable skills which are worth thinking about. The list below was drawn up by a team of four people in the United States and was written with young adults in mind. It is fascinating seeing how relevant it is to what we have said about narrative in general:

- *Play* is the capacity to experiment with one's surroundings as a form of problem-solving. It is self-chosen and hands-on and usually done to raise or answer a question or follow up an interest, a passion or a concern.

- *Performance* is defined as the ability to adopt alternative identities for the purpose of improvisation and discovery. We would call it role play.

- *Simulation* is the ability to interpret and construct dynamic models of real-world processes. We find children making models of things that interest them in the real world – often things with moving parts.

- *Appropriation* is the ability to sample and remix media content meaningfully. Kress talks of this when he says that children, in their meaning making, never copy but transform.

- *Multitasking* is the ability to scan one's environment and shift focus so as to take note of salient details. People say that young children have a limited attention span. However, a child who is deeply involved in something only shifts attention to focus on a different aspect of whatever it was she was originally interested in. The important phrase here is 'deeply involved'.

- *Distributed Cognition* is the ability to interact meaningfully with tools that expand mental capacities. Books are, perhaps, the supreme example of cognitive tools that expand our thinking – but what about computers?

- *Collective Intelligence* is the ability to pool knowledge and compare notes with others towards a common goal. Small children role playing are effective at pooling knowledge, negotiating who does what, changing tack when necessary and talking about what is happening.

- *Negotiation* is the ability to travel across diverse communities, noticing and respecting multiple perspectives, and grasping and following alternative norms. We have richly diverse groups in our classes and settings and they are learning about negotiation, communication, respect and difference.

- *Judgment* is not always fostered in early years classes and young children need help in becoming confident to make and express judgments. What is required is the ability to evaluate the reliability and credibility of different information sources. Helping children learn that they can choose between alternatives, express their own preferences, make choices and decisions is essential.

- *Transmedia Navigation* is the ability to follow the flow of stories and information across multiple modalities. Some years ago a little girl in an inner London nursery class drew pictures of a film she had seen at the weekend. The film was *Beauty and the Beast*. She cut out pictures and stuck them in a book, then dictated a story for an adult to write. She started to sing a song from the film and added her own dance. Next day she came in and invited other children to join her in acting out the story. The day after that she asked more children to come to add music. Finally she told the teacher she wanted everyone in the school to come and watch her production. Had she had access to a film crew I daresay she would have demanded their help too. Young children are – as we have seen – adept at multimodality

■ *Networking* is the ability to search for, synthesize and disseminate information. Our young children are often better at this than adults.

(Purushotma *et al*, 2010)

## Building a culture and pedagogy based on narrative

You might have thought that little would be required of you other than to keep up to date about what children's culture is and to mention it every so often or invite children to share aspects of it with you. But your heart might have sunk when reading the list above. If children are required to learn all of that your role requires more:

■ Know what children are currently interested in out of school. Ensure that you think carefully about what has mass appeal but also about aspects of popular culture that interest the children in your group, including those who may not have English as a first language

■ Watch what children do and listen to what they say particularly in the less formal sessions and times of the day – at playtimes, on outings, at dinner.

■ If you hear children say things or see them do things that cause you concern – bullying or mocking other children, teasing boys or girls for what they judge to be inappropriate gender responses, being violent or aggressive, making insulting comments about anyone's appearance or language don't ignore it. Don't say things like 'They are too young to know it is wrong' or 'They must have heard that at home' or 'It's not my job to deal with this'. You must deal with it. You must confront it in a way which shows them that you will not accept such behaviour. You are setting up rules for the accepted norms and appropriate behaviour for your little community.

■ When you talk to children about aspects of popular culture which you find offensive such as stereotyping or the use of inappropriate images of girls or boys try and get them to think about what it would feel like if that were applied to them or those they love. You are enabling them to become critical of these things. You are not seeking to ban or forbid them. What you are wanting to do is to help children learn that by thinking about things, making comparisons, talking to other people, thinking about stories they have heard and about their own experience, they can start to decide if something is good or bad, right or wrong.

# 8

## Children's books in translation

| cada otono | every fall |
|---|---|
| los nopales | the nopales |
| de mi casa | around my house |
| y del barrio | are laden with |
| se llenan | prickly pears. |
| de tunas | |

(from *Mi abuelita es como en nopal en flor*
by Francisco Alarcon)

Robert Frost is purported to have said 'Poetry is what is lost in translation', whilst Francis Grose said that translators were like sellers of old mended shoes and boots, somewhere between cobblers, or menders, and shoemakers, or creators. Both statements please me because they address the difficulties of translation and highlight how sensitive and nuanced translations have to be to succeed. For Frost the poetry is lost: for Grose the task of translator is impossibly situated between the creative and the restorative.

Many children's books are professionally translated from one language into another. In the UK the paucity of books in translation led individuals and groups attempting their own translations to find materials which speak to children in their home languages in schools and settings. This chapter explores some of these issues.

### The complex task of the translator

We are operating within a broad definition of literature, to encompass stories seen, read and heard. We will be looking at how these can be translated.

Lennart Hellsing, Swedish poet and author of children's books, also sees literature as everything that carries narrative. So for him plays, puppets shows, TV programmes, video games, films, DVDs and radio are as important as books in terms of children's learning and development. It is through all these things that children make meaning and gain access to the thoughts and ideas of others and to real and possible worlds. In this global digital world much of this is accomplished by translation from one language to another, from one medium to another.

The two most common ways of translating on screen are subtitling and dubbing. Although subtitling is the cheaper option, dubbing is the preferred choice when translating for a young audience since it does not depend on the rate of reading, which is likely to be very variable among young children. The job of the subtitle translator is initially to match the lip and mouth movements of the speaker to the words or phrases being said. The translator has to pay attention to the number of syllables in a word and the length of sentences. The main task is to make the meaning clear.

Translation cannot be literal, as where each word is translated regardless of context. You may well have encountered examples of this in your travels abroad or in emails from friends for whom English is not their first language. A friend told me of finding a sign in a Paris shop offering 'Dresses for street walking', and a sign in a hotel bedroom reading 'The manager has personally passed all the water in this hotel'. Each word might be a literal translation but the meaning is corrupted.

When a film or book is translated, more than words need to be made comprehensible. Cultural tools like books and films encapsulate ideas, views, attitudes and values of the makers and are thus rooted in the maker's culture and language. To be true to these ideas and values and made accessible to those with and from different languages and cultures, a transformation has to be made. That is why translation is such a difficult, nuanced and sensitive thing to do successfully.

Let us start with the simplest aspects of translating books and attempt to translate a few sentences from one language into another, remembering that the job of the translator is to convey the meaning.

Here is a page from *Lima's Read Hot Chilli* translated first into French and then into Russian.

> So Lima swallowed a whole glass of cold cold water
> Which was nice...
> But her mouth was still too hot!

*Alors Lima avala un verre entier d'eau froide*
*Ce qui etait bon...*
*Mais sa bouch etait toujours en feu!*

Так Лима заглютало все стекло холодной холодной воды которая была славна... но ее рот был все еще слишком горяч!

NOTE: I copied the French translation from my dual text edition where the translator was Annie Arnold. I copied the Russian translation from an online translation site. I then sent the copied translation to my Russian speaking daughter for her re-translation into English. Here is her translation 'so Lima swallowed the whole glass (although that's not the right word for 'a glass') of cold cold water which was (I think the word is glorious, but it's more like glory to the state)... but her mouth was still too hot.

All three of these languages fall into the Indo-European group, which is the world's largest language group and include languages like English (a Germanic language), French (a Romance language) and Russian (A Slavic language). On the simplest level it is apparent that the person translating from English to Russian has to deal with a different alphabet – the Cyrillic alphabet. A translator translating from English to Hebrew or Arabic would have to consider a different alphabet plus the different direction of print. Text is written and read from right to left in these language. And Hebrew may be written without vowels. Mandarin, which is the most widely spoken language of China and the one regarded as standard, is written with thousands of distinctive characters called ideographs. More than that the spoken language is tonal which means that meaning is dependent on tone.

In all their activities and situations children work to make and then share meaning What translators must do is take already created meaning and transform or re-form it to make is meaningful to others from different languages and cultures.

## Reviewing culture and cultural tools

Vygotsky saw culture as the result of groups in society constructing shared values, ideologies, religions, artefacts, customs and practices which then come to define and link them to one another. When he started thinking about how children learn, he talked of how they assign meaning. His emphasis was on the context within which this happens, highlighting the importance of the social and cultural worlds in all human learning and development. For him all learning was social. He meant social in the sense that ideas and concepts are often mediated by more experienced learners; that learning takes place in a context which may well be social in origin; that all learning builds on previous learning; and that learning takes place primarily through cultural and psychological tools.

Mediation is a crucial concept in understanding the process of meaning making. It refers to the use of cultural tools or signs to bring about qualitative changes in thinking. So we can talk of mediation as the use of communicable systems for representing reality as well as for acting on it. Communicable systems are ways of sharing thoughts and ideas: language is one such *communicable system*. So mediation is the use of ways of communicating, primarily through signs and symbols, in order to understand, explain or represent the world and our experiences in it. The initial discussion of signs and symbols, introduced in the chapter on semiotics, requires some further clarification and elaboration.

■ A sign stands for or represents an object or idea. In our culture a triangular road sign stands for danger. We share an understanding of this through our experience of encountering such signs.

■ A symbol also stands for or represents an object or a concept. The symbol for email is universal. The letters h/a/t represent the thing that people wear on their heads for warmth, protection or beauty. Each letter is a symbol. The symbol 13 stands for the number thirteen.

Human beings have developed many different ways of communicating their thoughts and ideas about the world. Often they have used signs and symbols in their communicative systems. As they develop ways of communicating, these very ways change thinking and understanding. For example, a film, which is not reality but a series of moving images sometimes bound by language and used to represent aspects of reality, can change thinking. The film is an artefact built up of signs and symbols. Change can come through reading a book, talking to a friend, seeing a play, looking at a painting, hearing music or listening to a lecture. So the ways of communicating, which can be called cultural tools, change the ways in which we think. One of the most important facts about cultural tools is that they allow us to think about things when the things themselves are no longer present. We can remember a film we watched in the cinema last night, or a book we read last summer or a talk we had with a friend weeks ago. There is clearly a link between thought, cultural tools and memory. So a book, a film, a graphic novel, a song or a story each derive from within a culture and reflect the values, principles, ideas and rituals of that culture.

When the cultural tool involves language the language itself carries the culture. If the cultural tools involve sounds, like music without words, there is cultural underpinning, but nothing that can be directly translated. There are many genres of music, all developed from and rooted in their cultures, but almost all are accessible to those willing to listen. Music can be repeated and transformed. There appear to be few known alternatives to music notation. What would be translated?

We cannot translate art which is situated in and reflective of culture. We can look at and admire and interpret what we see. On the surface art seems to be open to everyone and culture-free. Is this really so?

Aboriginal paintings, for example, clearly reflect the culture of the artists. They are made up largely of symbols which can be applied on a surface, object or the human body. It is believed that they give power to the object or person decorated and that they tell stories. For example a *Water Dreaming* painting might show the shape for a man, which is a U shape, sitting next to concentric circles which represent a water hole. So we might say that the painter is telling the story of how man can invoke rain. Sighted people make meaning from pictures or art without needing translation.

But we may need to know more to really make sense of what we see: knowing more enhances our meaning making. I recently visited an exhibition of modern Australian art in Sydney with a young artist friend. As we looked at the paintings her observations, rooted in her culture and that of the artist, enabled me to see things in the paintings that I might not otherwise have noticed. Perhaps music and painting are almost universal symbolic and semiotic systems.

A book or a story in one language cannot make sense to someone who does not know and understand that language. So that book or story needs to be translated into the language of the reader, listener or learner. When a book written within one culture is translated, what happens to the culture? Can culture be translated? That is the question which concerns us in this chapter.

## Reading and translating picturebooks as a semiotic process

Any translator starts work as a reader. The translator of a picturebook starts as reader and interpreter of both words and pictures.

The Russian philosopher Mikhail Bakhtin (1990) was concerned with the dialogic nature of both language and literature. What he meant is that is that any reading or language experience consists not only of words or text but also of all that has gone before and all that is yet to come. So a book refers back to the culture which created it, but also creates something new in the process of being understood and interpreted. Bakhtin introduced the concept of *heteroglossia* which means more than one voice. Within any written text there are examples of styles of language or uses of words and phrases which have particular meaning within a context. In Bakhtin's words

> At any given time, in any given place, there will be a set of conditions – social, historical, meteorological, physiological – that will ensure that a word uttered in that place and at that time will have a meaning different than it would have under any other conditions. (Bakhtin, 1990:428)

In a picturebook the pictures and words, which are both signs, are part of the context of the book and make the meaning. Changing one changes the whole context.

Translating the words and the pictures of picturebooks may also be understood as a semiotic process. In any picturebook a word, an image, a page, a double-page spread, the endpapers, the fonts, can all be seen as signs. Everything in a book is of importance. Every detail carries meanings, which have to be interpreted and represented by the translator. And it is apparent that there are many visual and cultural signs that the translator must be attuned to – the reading direction, the progress of the story over the pages, the significance of colours, the specific cultural features and so on.

Charles Peirce, sometimes called the father of semiotics, talked of three orders of signs: icon, index, and symbol.

- An icon is a sign of likeness; like a photograph, a portrait or a realistic visual representation.
- An index is a sign that is in a causal relationship to its referent, like smoke implying fire.
- A symbol is an invented, unrelated artificial sign: words are symbols so in English, for example, the word 'hat' does not look like a hat and probably originated from an earlier word for cover or protect.

All these different signs can be found in picturebooks. In Lee's book *Wave* the figure of the child is an icon in the sense that is a realistic representation of a small child. The wave itself is both an icon and an index. It looks like a wave but it also suggests power and strength. The only symbol is the word which is the title of the book. It is the relationship between all the aspects, all the signs, that influences the translator's choice of words and layout and use of pictures. It is in this sense that translating picturebooks is sometimes known as inter-semiotic translation (Davies and Oittinen, 2008).

## The challenge of translating picturebooks

*Granpa* by John Burningham is a made of a series of episodes between the little girl, Emily and her grandfather. They are seen on a beach, in a greenhouse, sitting at home. Each double page spread has full colour pictures painted in a naive and child-like style and the narrative is conveyed through the expressions on their faces, the sepia pictures from the old man's past and the child's imagination. Different typefaces indicate the voices of the two speakers. There is no narrator, no explanatory commentary and no regular sequence of events other than that of seeming to follow the seasons of the year. There is often a large gap between the text and the pictures. This means that the reader can make more of the story than what is in the text. The book ends with a picture of an empty chair and the old man's dog. It is up to the reader or beholder to decide what happened, and how the story ends.

We look at two translations of this book – one to film and one into German.

The animated film was made in 1989, hand-illustrated with coloured pencil in the style of the Burningham book. Accompanying the film was a musical score, and professional actors voiced the parts of Grandpa and Emily. Despite winning several awards, including the coveted *Prix Jeunesse* international award for excellence in children's television, it was never released as a DVD and did not become as popular as many other animated films, despite – or perhaps – because of its relative faithfulness to the book. One of the things the film did change was the ending and this happened because the directors felt that the stark ending of the original would not be palatable to a child audience. Making the ending 'happy' is a way of sanitising and prettifying reality and occurs frequently when difficult themes, addressed in children's books, are eliminated in other media. Death is an issue that preoccupies children. When adults maintain silence about it children are denied the opportunity to talk about or experience its impact safely through narrative.

In the German translation *Granpa* has become *Mein Opa und Ich* – literally *My Grandpa and Me*, suggesting that Emily is at the centre of the tale. On the cover the name of the author and the translator are given equal prominence. This is unusual in children's literature and may be because the translator, Irina Koschunow is herself an author of children's books. The dialogue running through the original is here replaced by text, all of it told in the past tense, prefiguring the ending. The tone is sentimental.

In her detailed critique of this book in translation Emer O'Sullivan (1998) states that the pictures have been downgraded, as where there is an unnecessary caption to a picture when the picture effectively provides the text.

Burningham's sensitive and meaning-laden pictures are thus reduced to mere illustrations. On the last page of the English book there is an eloquent absence of text: in the translated version the translator cannot resist filling in the silence. This leaves no room for sorrow and grief.

The translation seems to reflect a culture where children cannot be trusted to make their own meanings and need to have them fed to them through the text. In fact this translation had its license withdrawn and was subsequently replaced by a German translation regarded as truer to the original.

*Papa Vroum* was translated into English from the French as *Night Ride* and this American translation shows how the whole character of a picturebook can be altered by insensitivity and disrespect for the underpinning cultural values of the original. In the original story Gabriel and his father get stuck in traffic in their van and spend the night there. Whilst the father is asleep Gabriel believes he is in charge of driving the car and is visited by a number of animals. The focus of the narrative is Gabriel – his ideas, thoughts and imaginings which we learn about through his words. O'Sullivan (1998) notes that in the translation, Gabriel's voice disappears, to be replaced by a bland and anonymous commentary. So where the French text says:

> *Il ouvre la portiere et regarde.*
> *'Moins de bruit, les petits chats,*
> *Papa dort'*

which can be translated as

> He opened the door and looked out.
> 'Less noise, little cats,
> Papa is sleeping'

is replaced in the American version by:

> He opened the door and looked out.
> There were three kittens all by themselves in the parking lot.
> They were too little to have made that sound.

This text is set below an illustration clearly showing a monkey jumping onto the car from a vehicle in front of their van thus offering the meaning-making reader the opportunity to decide what made the noise. No child really needs the over-complicated explanation to what is both evident and humorous in the pictures.

From these two examples it is apparent that there are different views of children, of childhood and of the role of books within cultures. The French writer hands much of the control to the child, seeing the implied reader as competent at being able to use different cues to make meaning. The American view seems to be that of the dependent child, having to have everything clearly spelled out in words, denying the importance of the visual and restricting the meaning making possibilities.

## Translation and identity

When I started researching children's literature for this book I went back to the work of Allan and Janet Ahlberg which had so delighted me and my babies over forty years ago. They are wonderful and inventive books which pay attention to class as a serious issue in Britain – think about *Burglar Bill*; are full of links to a possibly shared cultural past, as in *Each Peach Pear Plum*; contain reminders of all the things that can be read – witness the brilliantly inventive *The Jolly Postman*; and reflect the everyday shared experiences of children, as shown in *Starting School*.

Yet there is something very English and very nostalgic about the books and I begin to wonder how accessible they are to some of our children. Meek (2001) celebrates how books can induct children into aspects of English culture. She also talks of books in translation where children encounter many and different narrative traditions which can help them develop their identities as members of different cultural groups and narrators of their own cultural stories. We all have identities which define us as both unique and as members of different groups – a family, a neighbourhood and a class.

Black children in apartheid South Africa had their first languages suppressed and their cultures worse than denigrated. Their self images were severely damaged. Where children are able to find aspects of their language and culture being explicitly celebrated in their schools and settings their sense of self is likely to be both strong and positive.

Much has been written about how children become able to live in several worlds at the same time. Gregory and Biarnes (1994) use the term 'syncretic' to describe what they call the creative transformation of culture – how people, including children, reinvent culture, drawing on their resources old and new. Children are members of various cultural and linguistic groups and actively seek to belong to them in ways which are not linear but dynamic, fluid and changing. Children do not remain in the separate world defined by their culture or group but move between these worlds. According to Kenner and Kress (2003) they live in 'simultaneous worlds'. So any child you encounter will be a member of the classroom or setting group, a member of the home and family group, a member of the community and street group and a member of the playground or peer group – and maybe others. As children become members of different groups they syncretise, or transform the languages and narrative styles, the role relationships and learning styles appropriate to each group and then transform the cultures and languages they use to create new forms (Gregory *et al*, 2004). Once again we see children not copying but always transforming.

Raymonde Sneddon (2009) presents wonderful examples of the ways in which the children in her study draw on the whole of their culture when reading and writing. When Lek and Durkan read a Turkish book together they came across the word 'salgam' and when Sneddon asked what 'salgam' meant they told her it was a turnip and were reminded tof a traditional Turkish drink.

| Lek: | It's a turnip and sometimes Turkish people turn the turnip, they do something with another fruit, I don't know and they just put it together and they squeeze it and... |
| --- | --- |
| Durkan: | A drink...And they put, children can drink it but it's a little bit hot, it's a little bit... |
| RS: | Is it strong? |
| Durkan: | No, it's a little bit like... |
| Lek: | It's a little bit thing, like, it's bad. |
| RS: | Is it bitter? |
| Durkan: | No it's hot. |
| RS: | Is it spicy? |
| Lek: | Spicy... |
| Lek: | They get, they put it in the machine, like four turnips and they squeeze and it, it turns, it goes in a special machine so they can take the germs and things out, and sometimes they clean it and put in a factory and then they take it to shops and people buy it. (Sneddon, 2009:111) |

Later in the same session Lek talked about the Turkish books he had at home and read with his mother, and then boasted of all the rhymes his grandmother was teaching him. The session ended with the children singing Turkish songs together, clapping the intricate rhythms that underpin them.

## The pleasures and potential problems of dual text books

Books where two languages appear on the same spread are becoming more widely available. They are referred to as dual text or dual language books. The making of such books in this country apparently first came about when teachers working with inner city children could not find books in languages other than English and started making their own books in English plus another language in order that the children could take these books home to share with their families. As long ago as the 1970s many educators were aware of the importance of recognising and celebrating the cultures and languages of the children in their groups. At around that time Eve Gregory at the Newham Women's Community Writing Group started to produce black and white picturebooks in the languages of the borough's children. Forty years on publishers such as Mantra Lingua and Roy Yates Books, specialise in dual language books for young children. For more information on dual text books consult the website developed at the University of East London http://www.uel.ac.uk/education/ research/duallanguagebook/.

There is much to be said that is positive about the use of dual language texts in classrooms and settings but also much to be concerned about, including:

- the tendency in translating from one culture to another to change the meaning in subtle and sometimes not so subtle ways – such as in softening dark endings or altering the positional role of the characters in the story

- the problem of deciding which language should come first and the messages given by this. Where English books are translated many educationalists would like to see the target language rather than the source language come first. Nathenson-Mejia and Escamilla (2003) have written about how, in their teacher training programmes in America, they induct trainee teachers into being critical readers of bilingual or dual text books in their work with Latino children. They comment:

> We learned that there is a difference between books that are published with each language in its own edition and those in which the two languages are in the same book. When each language is in a different book, everything else remains the same: illustrations, formats and fonts. However, when both languages are in the same book subtle differences make it difficult for some readers, usually those reading in Spanish. In most of the dual-language books, the Spanish is underneath the English, in a font (such as italics) that is more difficult for children to read,

and sometimes in a colour, such as blue) that is more difficult to see
...The placement of Spanish below the English (as it was in most of the
bilingual books) reinforces the lower status that Spanish occupies in the
dominant U.S. culture. (p107)

■ the issue of how the pages and the text on the pages and the direction
of movement through the narrative should appear where the target
language is read in a different direction from the source language.
One book maker has found an ingenious solution to this problem;
Jeannie Baker uses collage to produce fascinating images in books,
often about aspects of the natural world. She says the pictures start
off as drawings which become the guide for the collages that follow,
constructed layer by layer on a wooden baseboard out of natural and
artificial materials such as sand, earth, paints, wool, fabric and tin.
The collages are photographed to become the pages of the book.

In 2010 Baker made a book specifically to reflect on the similarities and differences between two families – one a family in her home city of Sydney, Australia and the other a family in the Valley of Roses in southern Morocco. Her
purpose was to explore what she calls the 'inner person' of individuals and
how this may be very different from outward perceptions. The first language
of her home community is English which is written from left to write, top to
bottom of the page. The first language of Valley of the Roses is Arabic which is
read from right to left. One of her aims was to eliminate the issue of which
language should come first. Another was to respect the direction of print together with the direction of the narrative.

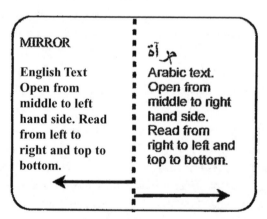

The book, *Mirror,* was published by Walker Books and supported by funding
from the Australian Government through the Australian Council, its funding

and advisory board. Baker's solution was to make a book which opens from the middle out as illustrated above. The arrows indicate the direction of print and narrative. It is a clever solution, although I fear expensive to produce. The English pictures and narrative occupies all the pages on the left side of the book, the Arabic pictures and narrative the pages on the right.

- the use of intertextuality or reference to traditional rhymes, stories or songs where some children might find making the connections difficult. Think about how a Polish child might struggle with understanding the references to English nursery rhymes and tales in *Each, Peach, Pear, Plum.*

- the difficulty of translating alliteration or rhyme, jokes and humour or metaphor from one language to another.

## The themes explored

Many books are translated from one language or format to another and they cover a wide range of themes. Many contain good narratives and often show positive images of other countries and cultures but in reality not enough reflect the real issues, pleasures, problems and concerns of contemporary children. Many children are migrants and have no permanent home; some are regarded as illegal and live in fear of being deported; children may have their names changed because they are thought too difficult to write, read or pronounce; many children feel devalued by schools; many move from one country to another; others have to translate and interpret for their parents. It is important that we offer these children stories that reflect at least something from their reality. This is why some books dealing with deep issues are successfully translated from one language to another. *Journey to Joburg*, for example, has been translated into dozens of languages across all continents.

## The child's work

The child's work in the context of books in translation is, as always, to make meaning and, in doing so, to make links with prior experience, the language, rituals and values of the home and community and those depicted in the book. Children whose culture is being recognised will be empowered to reflect on aspects of their language and culture and, in a welcoming environment, to talk about and share them with adults and children. Where children are in environments using dual text books or books translated into their language they have opportunities to display their linguistic and cultural expertise publicly and share it with peers and adults.

Children for whom English is their first language also benefit from exposure to books in other languages. Handling, reading and sharing books in a variety of languages shows them that all languages carry meaning, can appear in books, can be written and read and deserve respect.

## Building a culture and pedagogy based on narrative

- The work of the adult is complex since it can mean making choices about things you may not really understand. Knowing which books have been translated is simple but knowing the literary quality of the translation is difficult unless you are fluent in language. The translation of picture-books is also difficult to assess and you will need to question whether the translated version is true to the original or whether it perhaps sanitises, softens or in other ways changes the cultural values of the original.

- In terms of dual text books you will need to be alert to how the direction of print and narrative is dealt with.

- It is worth considering which languages you are going to ensure are re-flected in your classroom and to think about how you can involve children in showing off their expertise to others.

- Similarly you need to be attentive to how children respond to the texts that are available in their home languages and think about how you can show them you are interested in what narratives they have read, heard, seen and experienced at home and in their community.

# Part 3
# Reading the world

# 9

## Controversy: the role and significance of postmodern picturebooks

Once upon a time, in the middle of winter, a Queen sat at a window and thought to herself: 'Oh, what wouldn't I give to have a child.' And her wish was granted for not long after a little daughter was born to her, with skin white as snow, lips and cheeks as red as blood and hair black as ebony.

You know the rest. The Queen dies, the King remarries and the stepmother – that archetypal figure – beautiful, vain and evil, admires herself day after day in her magic mirror which affirms her beauty. The child grows up and becomes beautiful, more beautiful than the stepmother. And when the mirror tells the stepmother this she cannot bear it and calls a huntsman to take the child into the forest and slay her. He, however, allows her to escape and she is eventually taken in by seven dwarves who love and care for her. She manages to defeat numerous attempts on her life but eventually eats a poisoned apple and falls into a deep and lasting sleep. It is only the kiss of the handsome prince which brings her back to life. And of course they live happily ever after. A fairy tale translated into dozens of languages, retold in numerous versions, made into films and musicals, subject of songs and much debate.

In *The Uses of Enchantment: the meaning and importance of fairy tales* (1976), Bettelheim analysed the themes of this story and other fairy tales in terms of Freud's ideas. What is of interest to us is how this draws our attention to the ways in which traditional tales deal with deep and controversial issues. In the snippet above we have a mother's longing for a child, the death of a mother, the arrival of a stepmother, the stepmother's jealousy of the child, attempted murder of the child by the stepmother, lack of a father's presence, and more.

He's about to melt them on his tongue when he notices that each flake is decorated with words and numbers. It isn't snow. It's newspaper!

I was about to give up when my brother suddenly shouted, "Let's go out for dinner."

"Good idea," said Mom. "I know just the place."

I panicked. I mean, I was still dressed like a turkey! In the house was bad enough—but outside?!

from David Macaulay's *Black and White*

Here are at least six themes of abiding concern to young children, all addressed through narrative, allowing the child to confront and examine them without consequences.

In *Where the Wild Things Are* Max, in trouble with his mother, escapes on a magical journey to a place where fierce yet tender creatures roll their terrible eyes and gnash their terrible teeth, but he tames them and they join in a wild and joyous dance. So Max has power and can then deal with his loneliness and return to his room where his dinner is waiting for him and, magically, is still hot. Perhaps it is the very power and independence referenced in the narrative that allow both Max and the reader to cope with negative feelings like anger with a mother. The book received both acclaim and censure because many people felt that it was too dark and disturbing to be used with young children. But children, generally, loved it and many of them – and their parents – knew it by heart through repeated readings.

Children's literature has been used by parents and teachers as a way of teaching and reinforcing the values and expectations of the cultures in which we live. We often find in the books and stories children who live in or return to the safety of families, manage through hard work or skill or the use of magic to outwit evil or overcome obstacles or achieve a goal, have adventures in real and possible worlds and enjoy the company of others. More recent literature allows children to think about some aspects of real and troubled lives, as we have seen. Some theorists believe that books which fall into the genre of *postmodern picturebooks* allow children to develop a greater awareness of this world and their roles in it, and thus give them permission to question which then empowers them.

## A literature to think with

Postmodern picturebooks, it is argued, are non-linear in structure and self-referential in that they keep reminding the reader that they are not fact but fiction, contained within the boundaries of a story or book. Linguists use the word metafiction to describe this quality. Some books already discussed fall into this genre including *Shhh* and books by Anthony Browne. So does David Macaulay's *Black and White* where the traditional technique of literal storytelling is abandoned so that the young reader is challenged to piece together four interconnected plots that unfold through the illustrations placed in separate quadrants on each two page-spread (see pages 110-111). On the opening pages the four split panes each offer a title:

| | |
|---|---|
| *Seeing things* | A WAITING GAME |
| Problem Parents | *Udder Chaos* |

At first sight the book is about everyday things like parents and cows and train trips and newspapers, but is it quite so simple? Macaulay himself tells children 'This books appears to contain a number of stories that do not necessarily occur at the same time. Then again, it may contain only one story. In any event, careful inspection of both words and pictures is recommended.'

Kathleen O'Neil (2010) discusses how postmodern picturebooks serve a different purpose from picturebooks of earlier times. Children's books in the last century largely presented idealised lives of middle class children with clearly defined roles for boys and girls, rich and poor, strong and weak, clever and not, as well as various stereotypes of 'other' people, that is: not white, not rich, not English. She suggests the literature of this century appears to be making some attempt to invite children to question certain prevailing assumptions, norms, stereotypes and expectations.

We saw this in *The Paperbag Princess* who is not a feeble, weak and vain creature waiting for her prince, but a strong and clever hero who solves her own problems, defeats her own dragons and lives an independent life. A long way from *Snow White*. A child hearing this story read and looking at the pictures is being invited to think about what is different about this story from what she might have expected. As Paula Geyh (2003), who teaches postmodern literature and theory at Yeshiva Univeristy says 'Postmodern literature, then, is literature to think with' (p12).

Most theorists agree that postmodern picturebooks are characterised by the following features:

- the *breaking of boundaries* which is equivalent to the non-traditional use of plot
- a sense of *parody*, or cynicism or irony
- *indeterminacy* which suggests something not clearly defined or fixed in stone, but vague and open to interpretation
- the expectation that the *reader/viewer/listener will actively have a role to play in the construction of the story not merely being a consumer of the story.*

Let us look for some examples, offered primarily by O'Neil.

Jon Scieszka re-tells the story of the *Three Little Pigs* but calls his 1989 version *The True Story of the 3 Little Pigs*. He tells the story from the point of view of the wolf and the listener or reader has to decide if the wolf is innocent or guilty. To do this the reader must identify with the wolf and the writer has to find ways of making that happen. Some questions arise. Things are not fixed or certain. Was all the wolf's huffing and puffing perhaps merely sneezing? Was he justified in eating one of the pigs who died when the house collapsed? After all, one should not waste. Towards the end of the story the news media appear and the reporters are clearly on the side of the pigs. Another question for the digital-wise, media-friendly child listener or reader: is this truth or is there bias? Does this question apply only to this story or to others we see on the news, read in the papers or hear people talk about at home? This is a question which is very relevant today.

Eugene Trivizas offers another version (2001), called the *Three Little Wolves and the Big Bad Pig,* in which the wolves are sweet and cuddly whilst the pig is a rude bully. Both these versions of a traditional tale conform to the four features of postmodern literature listed above. Both raise issues for thought, questioning and discussion.

## Decentering: taking someone else's point of view

One of the things Scieszka and Trivizas invite children to do is to think about what someone else thinks or feels – to consider a familiar story from the point of view of someone else. Piaget maintained that young children were unable to do this because he saw them as being egocentric. Although this was disproved by the work of Judy Dunn, Martin Hughes and others, many people still believe that young children cannot see the world from the perspective of another. Being able to decentre is very important to being able to analyse and understand people, their actions, feelings and motives. When authors impute or suggest rather than state motives and feelings, readers and listeners need to decentre to see the world from a range of viewpoints.

I remember being shocked when Brian Simons, then a teacher at an inner-city school in London, asked the 7 year old children in his class to draw up a petition for the rights of the poor troll whose life was being ruined by the greed of the three Billy Goats Gruff. The children quickly became involved in heated discussions about who was right and who was wrong and why. They were putting themselves in the shoes of someone else and considering what was fair and what was not. And this is a question that really concerns children – witness many a playground dispute. Simons, a gifted teacher with strong political views, used a traditional tale and shifted the emphasis to enable the children to think about the story in a different way.

As the subject matter for his book *Voices in the Park*, Anthony Browne takes an everyday and ordinary visit to the park by a mother and her son and a father and his daughter. Each event in the park is described four times as each parent and child gives their own version of what happened. Browne ensures that each has a distinctive voice and tone. This is an example of *heteroglossia*. Each character simply narrates what happens: nothing is added or invented. But what we get is the multi-layered reality which is at the heart of every event.

The first voice is that of the upper middle class mother who worries that her precious little boy has been playing with what seems to her a rough-looking little girl. Then the unemployed father describes how he spent the time at the park looking through the job adverts in the paper whilst his daughter and the dog played. The third voice is that of the little boy who remembers what fun he had playing with the girl in the park and finally, the fourth voice is that of the daughter of the unemployed man.

Layer upon layer of narrative and on top of that there are the layers of narrative in the pictures. On one page we see Father Christmas dancing on the path, followed by a couple doing the tango, the light bulb in the shape of a flower and King Kong standing atop a building. This is an extremely sophisticated book and children's responses are often revealing and fascinating. Ben delightedly pointed to the picture on the last page where the text reads, 'When I got home I put the flower in some water, and made Dad a nice cup of tea' and said 'I bet he put the flower in Dad's tea. Serve him right for being so fed up in the park'.

The book makes clear how one event can be experienced and felt differently by each person sharing it. It perfectly illustrates how postmodern picturebooks use indeterminacy to illustrate how things are often not fixed but vague and capable of being experienced and explained in different ways.

## Difference, othering and orientalism

Perry Nodelman, one of the foremost thinkers on children's literature, has drawn on the work of Edward Said, philosopher and writer, who examined Western attitudes towards Arabs and Asians to inform his thoughts on adult attitudes to children and childhood as revealed through children's literature. Said, in his seminal work *Orientalism* (1978), said that orientalism – how history, culture, and peoples of the east were described – could be paralleled with the ways in which corporate institutions deal with the East in order to dominate, control and restructure it. Intentions are linked to control and power. Nodelman suggests that we can apply this same approach to looking at how adults, who control child psychology and children's literature, do similar things. They make explicit and implicit statements about childhood and the expectations and norms within cultures applied to it. So they use children's literature to have authority over childhood. This view is troubling but worth thinking about.

It is clear that those who write children's literature and write about it, like me, are adults and we perpetuate our roles as speakers about children and on behalf of children. Nodelman argues that in doing this we impose on children a suggestion of their developmental or cognitive inferiority. We see them as not yet capable of certain things. Some would call the inability of children to speak for themselves innocence rather than ignorance, but the question arises as to whether this suggests a way in which we keep children naive and silent and thus 'other' them. We speak for them. Nodelman says, for example, that we produce a children's literature that is almost totally silent on the subject of sexuality, and it is unclear why this is so. By doing this we prevent children from being able to discuss sexuality with us even though there is growing evidence that issues around sexuality are of concern to many children.

Another concern of children which is often glossed over is the nature of 'the family'. There are many children in our schools and settings living in families other than traditional two different-sex parent families. There is a paucity of books in the UK which offer narratives about children from other than traditional families. And unless all children have access to seeing families like theirs represented in some way their opportunity to think about this aspect of diversity is restricted. In the USA more children's book are produced which deal with gender and sexuality. Leslea Newman has written several books relating to non traditional families including *Daddy, Papa and Me, Heather has Two Mommies* and *Mommy, Mama and Me* and whilst they may not be great literature they are making the unspoken spoken. Also from the United States come several books looking at still controversial aspects of gender. *My Prin-*

*cess Boy* by Kilodavis and DeSimone and *10,000 Dresses* by Ewart and Ray challenge gender roles and stereotypes. Offering books like these might cause controversy but could open the door to children who are beginning to feel they can talk about some of the issues that interest or concern them. The UK publishes books along similar lines, such as *Oliver Button is a Sissy* by Tomie de Paola, which is about gender stereotypes, name-calling and being teased.

Children are teased because of perceived difference on any grounds. There are still relatively few books which explore what it feels like to be teased or alienated because of culture or language. Those which do, do so in indirect ways. Among the most familiar are David McKee's *Elmer,* which examines the effect of being discriminated against on the basis of colour and Bernard Most's *The Cow That Went Oink* in which the cow that oinks and the pig that moos are jeered at by the other animals. Most's solution is to turn the teased animals into experts so they teach the other animals their languages. The question arises whether this soft approach is the only or best way of dealing with the many serious issues which affect children.

## Agency: being in control of your own actions and ideas

Young children often feel powerless. They are physically small and not very strong. They may not be confident in their own ideas or their right to express them. It is not so long ago that children were thought to be best 'seen and not heard' and although nowadays some feel that children are heard too much, developing a sense of agency is important in helping children understand that they can effect change. Despite being small, being children, they can be in control of their own ideas and actions. They need not be silent, invisible, complaint or passive. In many traditional tales, a child becomes the hero and manages to outwit the giant, or solve the riddles or find a way to leave a trail so as to be found. In *Where the Wild Things Are* Max is, in a sense, in control of his life – although the safe ending suggests that this is only in a dream.

Postmodern picturebooks often suggest that the accepted rules of behaviour can be changed, particularly when they are unfair. Again this opens the door to discussion about the possibilities of change. In *King & King* by Linda de Haan and Stern Nijland (2000) the social conventions of a man marrying a woman are turned on their head. The story goes like this. The queen's son needs a bride so she invites princesses from all over the kingdom to come to the castle. One of these princesses is accompanied by her older brother, act-ing as chaperone. The prince takes one look at the brother; they fall in love, marry, rule as king and king and, of course, live happily ever after. Since there are children living in various family groups it is important that they have their reality reflected. More than that it is important that social conventions are examined, discussed and challenged.

## A story within a story within a story

The word *metalepsis* is used to describe what writers, film makers or artists do when they embed one story or narrative within another and then another. Earlier in this book, we saw young Jacob use the analogy of Russian dolls to describe this feature in the book *Granny Torrelli Makes Soup*. The effect of this device of embedding one story within another is to make the narrative more complex so the reader, listener or viewer has to unpick and unravel to follow the thread to find the meanings.

Computer games or interactive fiction are constructed so reality and fiction are intertwined and the narrative goes in and out of the fictional world. More-over the boundaries between real and fictional may be blurred.

The Tamagotchi craze, first started in 1996, when children could make, nurture and rear a virtual and digital handheld pet. These pets, designed for children aged 8 or over, became so popular that they were played with by younger children and adults. The game – if we can call it that – starts with the pet hatching from its virtual egg, being given a gender and a name. The task of the player is to raise the Tamagotchi in good health, think about its needs, keep it happy through playing with it, keep it at a healthy weight, clean up its excrement, praise or punish it, medicate it when necessary, and put it to bed. Successful rearing allows the Tamagotchi to evolve from infancy to old age through the stages of life. It can find a partner in another Tamagotchi of the opposite gender – no alternatives possible here – and they can 'mate' and produce babies. The Tamagotchi culture ensures that each mating results in two babies, one of which is kept by the female and the other by the male.

The significant thing about the Tamagotchi is that it dies if not properly cared for. The potential possibilities for controversy are enormous. This creature, so real in many ways and so completely fictional in others, mixes reality with fiction in extraordinary ways and allows the child to meld her real life with the virtual life of the creature in her care. Two films and an animated series on Japanese TV have so far been made.

We have looked at how children using picturebooks pay attention to the fixed story which comes through the 'words on the page' and in the ear, and to the developing story in their heads which they make from the images. The two may contribute to or conflict with one another according to the intentions of the author/artist, the skills of the narrator and, most significantly, the needs and interests of the child.

Sylvia Panteleo (2010) takes three postmodern picturebooks to analyse in terms of metalepsis, the layers of meaning. The books are fascinating and only one is by an author/artist we have met before – Emily Gravett.

Her book *Wolves* won both the Kate Greenaway Medal and the Nestle Children's Book Prize Bronze Award in 2005 and in it she uses *wit and parody* and draws on the work of Allan Ahlberg in *The Jolly Postman* by incorporating texts from the real world into the fictional world. The book opens on a double page spread showing, on the left hand page, copyright information on a postcard where the message is Gravett's dedication to her son and where the stamp holds the image of a wolf. The facing page is a leaflet telling the reader that there is a new book in the library called *Wolves* written by Emily Grrrabbit. The cover of the this advertised book is identical in all other respects to the one the reader is holding. On the poster is a sticker reading 'Burrow WOLVES and many other rip-roaring tails at your local library NOW!' You will, in these few examples, have recognised the play on words and meanings Gravett employs.

Turn the page and we are in the library and the story starts. Rabbit picks a book called *Wolves* and when he opens his book there is an identical copy of the endpapers in the real book, only these look slightly more worn. Stuck on the left hand page is a library pocket holding a real borrowing card, on which are coffee stains and a wonderful little doodle on the back, and on the right hand side a date stamp sheet.

Rabbit starts to read the book and learns facts about wolves. So this seems to be a non-fiction book. As Rabbit gets more and more engrossed in the story going on in his head, some of which we deduce from the pictures, as in the one of the wolf dressed as grandma or the one of the wolf holding a knife and fork, we face a tragic ending. But on the middle pages we find a declaration that no rabbits were eaten in the making of the book and it is a work of fiction. There follows an alternative ending for more sensitive readers. Read it for yourselves!

So far we have found aspects of metafiction in Gravett's books, but she goes further and one of the devices she uses to great effect is called *mise-en-abyme*, where a visual or verbal text is embedded in another text, but in a miniature version. We see this, for example, on the page where the cover of the real book is replicated in miniature on the advertising leaflet in the library. *Mise-en-*

*abyme* also occurs at the narrative levels. We are reading a book called *Wolves* in which Rabbit is reading a book called *Wolves*. The boundaries between the real and the fictional worlds are blurred.

Pantaleo's analysis is more detailed than we have space for here. You can download it at www.springerlink.com/index/p9r517746559102k1.pd

In Ian Lendler's *An Undone Fairy Tale*, illustrated by Whitney Martin, we find many of the elements of the traditional fairy story. Here is how it begins:

> Once upon a time there lived a princess who was famous throughout the land. Not only was she beautiful, but she baked the most delicious pies in the king-dom. Many men wishes to marry her. But she was very lonely.
>
> You see, her stepfather, the king, loved her for only one reason – her pies.
>
> And to keep anyone else from having them, he locked her in a tall, dark tower.
>
> No one, not even her mother, could help her.

To have a stepfather rather than a stepmother and to be loved only for you pies are new variants on the traditional tale. The prospective suitors have to perform three dangerous tasks – as expected – and all fail – as expected. It is only when Sir Wilbur arrives and asks for the princess's hand in marriage that something unusual happens on the pages of the book. The king wears a doughnut instead of a crown, and we are told that this is because Ned, who is painting the pictures, can't keep up with the speed of the reader. Here we have a reminder that this is a story in a book and that a person has drawn – or is drawing – the pictures. The reader is asked not to turn the page because Ned has not yet finished painting the horses or the armour Sir Wilbur will need to carry out his first task of killing the dragon. This device of speaking directly to the reader whilst telling the tale continues throughout the book and Pantaleo tells us that this creates a secondary narrative. The reader is no longer outside the story but becomes directly involved in it through the action of reading too fast and turning the pages.

## Good intentions or authenticity of voice

So far in this chapter we have looked at themes which might be regarded as controversial, considered how children might be excluded by not finding their reality reflected in narratives, examined books which offer the possi-bility of adopting alternative viewpoints and, in passing, touched on various aspects of diversity. So far I have said nothing at all about power. Here I revisit some of the books already described to look again at the perspective they take – this time asking the important question: should the aim of multicultural children's literature be to promote cultural awareness and sensitivity, what we might call assimilationist pluralism, or should it also be concerned with depicting and illustrating the realities of who holds the power and why? In other words should children's literature be looking more carefully at authenticity in terms of whose voices we hear and how they address realities of power.

Of the books we have considered so far a fair number are cited by Stuart Ching (2005) as examples of pluralism. What he means is that they promote awareness of the importance of cultural differences and try to suggest a common humanity. They are good in intention. But for Ching they do not address power. The books cited include Most's *The Cow that Went Oink* and Eve Bunting's *Smoky Night.*

Another book on the list is Gary Paulsen's *The Tortilla Factory* and this offers a starting point for Ching's analysis. It is a beautifully illustrated, poetic account of how tortillas come to be made and it evokes a sense of the pastoral and the dignity of work as it traces the planting of yellow seeds by brown hands in black earth. The book romanticises labour by situating it in a idyllic and bucolic landscape. The labourers in the book have no voice. They are observed from outside. They are othered.

Ching offers us a contrast: Lenore Look's *Love as Strong as Ginger,* the story of the relationship between a Chinese American girl and her grandmother. The story, told using Taishanese, a dialect of Chinese, and drawing on the author's own memories of her Southeast Asian immigrant grandmother, does not shirk from describing the harsh conditions of the cannery. The author's note that introduces the book sets the scene graphically:

> This story was inspired by my grandmother who worked in a Seattle cannery in the 1960s and 1970s. She was among the older immigrant women, mostly from Southeast Asia, who, because they lacked English and job skills, did the only work they could find: shaking crab. The work paid very little: three pennies for crabmeat. (Look, 1999. Author's Note)

The authenticity of the voice used plus the recognition of the injustice faced are essential and unusual ingredients of a book for children.

*Nappy Hair* by Carolivia Herron is a book that has been the subject of much controversy. The author is an English professor. Her book is written in the African American epic tradition, using call and response as indicated in fonts of different sizes in the text, embedded blues lyrics and graphic and colourful language, as where Brenda's hair is described as the 'nappiest, fuzziest, the most screwed up, squeezed up, knotted up'. *Nappy Hair* was loved by the black and Latino children but surprisingly detested by many of their parents, who described it as reinforcing negative cultural stereotypes about being black. In fact the book is a celebration of difference, of self-respect and pride. A teacher who used it in her classroom was ousted from her school in Brooklyn because of the controversy. Yet sales of the book in the USA are described as still robust.

## Literature and identity

In this chapter we have been looking at issues related to identity. Who you are – your identity – is made up of many things: the language or languages you speak and perhaps read and write; where your family came from; the colour of your skin; your position in the family; your beliefs and values; your family structure; the school or college or university you went to and what your parents do. The key concept here is that of culture.

In *The Idea of Culture* (2000) Terry Eagleton agrees with Raymond Williams who said that culture was one of the two or three most complex words in the English language. Eagleton added to this by saying:

> Culture is not only what we live by. It is also, in great measure, what we live for. Affection, relationship, memory, kinship, place, community, emotional fulfill-ment, intellectual enjoyment, a sense of ultimate meanings; these are closer to us than charters of human rights or trade treaties. (p131)

Narratives, spoken, visual or written, deal with all these issues and through the making of narratives and engagement with them, children are able to explore and expand their sense of themselves as both unique and as part of com-munities. All this is obvious – for a child to be able to build her identity as a full member of the community of any class or setting she needs to find aspects of her language, culture and experience in the stories and books she encounters. It is important to take time and trouble to find out as much as possible about the languages, cultures and experiences of the children and to find books and stories to reflect them. In doing so you explicitly show respect for each child. An explicit recognition of language and culture is important for all children in a class or group since it gives them insights into what their peers have ex-perienced, know and value.

This chapter has discussed books that allow readers to think about issues often ignored by writers for children and some of the controversies which the publication and use of such books have given rise to. It is important to con-sider what it must feel like to encounter nothing from your own culture, life, experiences, values, feelings or fears in the books read and told to you. A last word on this comes from the chapter by Beverley Naidoo in Susan Lehr's *Battling Dragons*. Eleven-year-old Asma, living in London wrote to Beverley after she read *Journey to Jo'burg* asking:

> Why shouldn't young people learn what is really happening on Earth. I mean kids our age only learn about the good things, but we never learn the facts. The quicker we learn about the facts and forget fiction, the more intelligent and strong willing we shall become. That way we can make peace. (p37)

Naidoo wants us to use the power of fiction to explore serious and true things. She, alongside Morpurgo and others, urges educators and carers and those involved in the lives of young children to go back to narrative to offer children serious and honest, as well as humorous and jokey, material and encourage them to bring their own experience to this to think about, critique and discuss the issues that matter to them.

Some years ago research psychologists at Washington University used brain scans to examine cellular activity inside people's heads as they read stories. What they found is fascinating. They found that readers mentally replicate each new situation they encounter in a narrative: the neurons reproduce what would happen in reality in response to the fictional event. So, for example, if the reader reads of someone running away the neurons that control large muscle movements fire in the reader's brain. Moreover the actions and feelings in the story become interwoven with the reader's past experiences. Perhaps most significantly the strong emotions evoked by events in a narrative cause changes in brain function that have been shown to last beyond the reading. What Nicholas Carr (2011) calls 'deep reading', meaning losing oneself in a book, makes readers more empathetic and aware of the lives of others.

# 10

## Making the coin and currency:
## the child as narrator

Our jaws drop to our chests the evening
Abuelita steps out in a dress. Even the orange cat
glows its yellow eyes in surprise. Imagine that!
Abuelita waltzing out of the house in a shimmering
gray gown. Abuelita only wears pants and jeans.
(From *Abuelita Wears a Dress* by Rigoberto Gonzalez)

Narrative is about communication so for the child to become a narrator she has to acquire her first language or languages. A newborn infant immediately starts actively making sense of the world using senses and body movements. Making narrative sense requires being able to communicate with others who share a communicative framework like language.

This chapter begins with a brief overview of language acquisition.

### Acquiring a first language or languages

The fact that the human infant manages to acquire the vocabulary and grammar of her first language within the first year or so of life and without explicit lessons is one of the most startling cognitive feats and is much discussed and debated. For generations it was thought that language acquisition came about primarily through imitation and reward. It was the work of Noam Chomsky that first cast doubt on this. Chomsky, like many great thinkers, asked questions no one had asked before. He asked why it was that children said things they had never heard and how this were possible if all that was involved was imitation.

He observed that in the early stages of acquiring language children make few errors. But when they start paying attention to the patterns of what they hear and to use more complex language they begin to work out what seem to be the rules governing their language. They are generating a set of linguistic rules. At this stage they start to make errors and these errors are not things they have heard fluent speakers of the language say. This means they are learning through more than imitation. As they work out the rules they over-apply them. For example, one of the rules of English grammar is that plurals end with 's' and young children often say 'childs' instead of children, 'sheeps' instead of sheep or 'mans' instead of men. Another rule in English is to add 'ed' to the end of verbs to put them in the past tense. So we hear young children say 'the bird flied', 'the dog goed' or 'the 'boy feeled'. We know from our experience that the rules do not always apply: there are exceptions – but young children do not know that yet.

For Chomsky this was evidence that children were born pre-programmed to notice that there are rules holding spoken language together. This realisation makes them work out the rules and then apply them to everything before re-cognising that there are certain exceptions to the rules.

Bruner agreed with much of this much of this but thought that Chomsky failed to pay enough attention to the context – to the role of culture and the social in language acquisition. Through observing infants and young children, Bruner had noticed the importance of the routinised interactions that took place daily between the human infant and caregiver (usually the mother) and always involving language – what he called *formats*.

## The beginnings of making meaning

Bruner is certain that children's acquisition of language is essentially inter-active and social and requires the modelling and interaction of caregivers. He sees the formats as being the real preparation for narration. According to his analysis, what happens is that:

■ The formats take place during *real life at home activities where the adult can and does highlight the features of the world that are known and important to the child*. When doing this the adult instinctively uses simple grammatical forms. An example would be the adult lifting the child up from sleep, saying something like 'upsadaisy' to accompany the action. The child is lifted from sleep by the adult telling the child over and over what she is doing.

- *The adult helps the child by encouraging and modelling lexical and phrasal substitutes for familiar gestural and vocal means.* An example would be the baby looking at an apple and making a sound. The adult, following the child's gaze, interprets the sound as a request and asks 'Do you want an apple?'

- When the *child, in play, enters pretend mode the adult can join in and listen and respond to what the child does with the tone of voice, the inflection and intonation and grammar and vocabulary of the roles* they are playing.

- *Through experience the routinised formats can be generalised* so that child and caregiver can engage in shared or joint activities.

Bruner argued that learning language involves more than watching and listening: it involves doing. So learning language is learning how to get things done with words. This implies that the child is not only learning what to say but how to say it, who to say it to and under what circumstances.

Bruner is also certain that the child has in place some communicative function or intention long before being able to produce and use language. Such intentions include learning how to share attention with someone, take turns and name or refer to things. So it is clear that language acquisition is deeply context bound and Bruner cites evidence that children who understand context can also understand appropriate aspects of grammar.

He suggests that language acquisition is greatly aided by the child, in some prelinguistic way, being able to understand either the significance of what other people are talking about or the situation where the talk is happening. The question he asks is how this can happen. How does a child understand the significance of what is happening in a way that can help her learn the associated vocabulary and grammar? His explanation is that it is all to do with the child understanding the context and the function of language. The child cannot possibly learn language through rote or by simply listening and watching, only through using it in context.

This is all complicated and difficult to explain and understand. In essence what we need to know is that children come to language through having a sensitivity to context and to the uses of language in context. To explain and illustrate this Bruner emphasised the importance of the interactive and predictive games, or formats, between a human infant and the mother or other primary caregiver. These include peekaboo games where one or other is hidden and then revealed – a routine which is repeated again and again and bathed in language. The child becomes able to work out several things: the intention of the adult, a prediction of what will happen next and the ability to join in. So the child, whilst mastering and collaborating in prelinguistic games, is developing *a theory of mind* – the ability to understand the thoughts, intentions and feelings of others. The ability develops and is essential to becoming attuned to the social world and language acquisition. It underpins the ability to become a member of the world of narration. Bruner calls this *entry into meaning.*

## Becoming a narrator

Bruner asks what a child needs to know and do in order to become a narrator and believes that there are four grammatical constituents to consider.

- The first is the means for emphasising what is called '*agency*': by wich I mean actions aimed at goals. A narrative must have someone or something working towards achieving a goal. The cow that oinks wants to be accepted by the others; the handsome prince wants to marry the beautiful princess; Hansel wants someone to be able follow the trail he leaves behind.

- The second is the ability to organise events in a or logical or *sequential order* and to maintain that order. When young children start telling their protonarratives each might consist of one event. 'I saw a dog'. As the child becomes more expert one event is joined to another in a linear fashion: 'I saw a dog and it barked and I was scared and I ran away and I fell and I cut my knee'. The wonderful little word 'and' miraculously allows the novice narrator to link happenings in an ever-growing story chain. It is only with experience of different forms of stories read and told that young narrators become able to reflect back and look ahead within the logic of the narrative sequence.

  > When 7 year old Thabo tells a story: 'Last night I had a strange dream. In it I flew over the mountains to a place where it was always day. I hope I fly again in my dream tomorrow', he can reflect back (last night) and look ahead (I hope to). He has become able to do this through experience in daily life and from listening from stories read and told.

- The third is the awareness of and sensitivity to what Bruner calls *canonical* – knowing and respecting the accepted and straightforward ways of telling stories or the rules of narrative. We have seen how children's first way of creating strings of sequences is through using the connective 'and'; later they use words like 'then' and 'after that'. Later still they use causals, words or phrases like 'because of' or 'owing to'. Here is 6 year old Tamara's story:

128

One night I saw a kangaroo dancing around a circle and I shouted as loud as I could but she couldn't hear. So I touched her. She saw me. Then she changed her mind and came closer to me. In the end, because she was scared, she ran away. (Smid, 1998:164)

■ The last of the constituents is *voice*. Almost all narratives require the perspective or point of view of the teller of the tale. Consider how, in a powerful novel called *Room* by Emma Donaghue, the voices of the mother and child each tell the story of being locked in a room and breaking out of it. The two voices are strongly contrasted, linked into a reflection of the incredible bond between mother and child. Each voice offers a different perspective of events.

## Narrative and discourse

To understand what Bruner is saying about the importance of narrative it is important to understand what he means by *discourse*. The French philosopher and social historian Michael Foucault described discourse as the patterns of language that tell us more than what the words alone imply. What we hear or read allows us to analyse the culture the person using the language is part of, the network of social institutions she is involved with and possibly even the assumptions she holds. Foucault believed that discourse operates in four ways:

■ It can be thought of as creating a world, a virtual world which we construct through our complex interactions with one another, and between our experience, education and background. So discourse, in the form of the chains of language that bind us to others, *plays a key role in the social construction of reality.*

■ It can *generate both knowledge and truth.* Knowledge is not just communicated through language: it is constructed by us and organised through language itself.

■ Discourse *tells us about the people who speak and write it.* We have touched on how it is adults who primarily write for children and so assume a role of authority. Similarly people who write about literature, psychology or education often choose to write in a language which states their power and authority.

■ It follows that discourse is *intimately involved with socially embedded networks of power.* Think of how small we feel when faced by legal jargon, medical terminology or even the writings of people like me. The particular language developed by professions allows those within it a shorthand way of sharing knowledge but also acts as gatekeeper, ensuring that anyone outside that culture, group or profession are kept out.

Let us look at what some professional narrators do in terms of discourse, not through a formal framework of discourse analysis but in terms of what the sample of narrative chosen allows me to assume about the author. Try it for yourselves to see if we agree. It would be unfair to ask you to name authors or books but try situating each passage in a time and place.

1. A small breakfast-room adjoined the dining-room. I slipped in there. It contained a bookcase: I soon possessed myself of a volume, taking care that it should be one stored with pictures. I mounted into the window-seat: gathering up my feet, I sat cross-legged, like a Turk; and having drawn the red moreen curtain nearly close, I was shrined in double retirement

2 Sold your momma for a nickel.
> Yes, Lord, they did it.

And your daddy for a dime.
> Yep.

I say they sold your momma for a buffalo.
> That's the way it was.

And your daddy, they sold him for one thin dime.
> That's what they did.

But this nap come riding express,
coming on across the ocean from Africa,
wouldn't stop for nothing.

3 At this, the animals fell silent.

Then the elephant spoke. 'The damage is done,' he said sadly. 'We can never be friends again. From now on we shall be enemies: the cock and the bush cat, the antelope and the leopard, the zebra and the lion, and myself and man.'

Then all the animals turned and disappeared into the bush.

Some things are evident. The three voices and styles of writing are very different.

■ The style of writing of the first example is more formal and old-fashioned in both grammar and vocabulary (moreen) than the other two. It is from Charlotte Bronte's *Jane Eyre*.

■ The second was written by someone familiar with call and response stories using a lilting and hypnotic style, peppered with unfamiliar words and what might seem incorrect English forms. It comes from the black American author Carolivia Herron's *Nappy Hair*.

■ The writing of the last one follows a style familiar in books with cumulative texts for young children. This is evident in the list of animals, hinting at what had happened to each over the previous pages. It is from *The Honey Hunters*, by Francesca Martin.

It is possible to do the same thing for the three bits of narrative below, only this time they are narratives made by children. They can be analysed to see what can be found out about the narrator but it is important to focus on meaning and not surface features, like grammar and spelling. The questions to ask concern what the narrator is drawing on and how each piece can legitimately be called narration. This is the first:

Once upon a time there was a wolf and he wanted to play with a boy but the boys dad told him not to talk to strangers so he ran off and the wolf came to a bird but it just flew off as well then came to another wolf and they made friends and they lived together happy ever after. (Daniel, cited in Bearne, 1994:88)

This is the second:

Once there was a man and a mother and two sisters and a brother. First the oldest sister ran away. Then the second sister decided to stay home with the father but he ran away too. So the little brother and the sister were left and she learned how to cook. One day a lion came because she wished for a lion and also they lived in the jungle. He said, 'Can I be your pet?' She said 'I was just wishing for a lion pet. You can carry us wherever you want.' So they lived happily ever after. (Wally, from Paley, 1981:12-13)

And this is the third:

Once upon a time, in a faraway kingdom, there were lots of big houses and there were some very, very pretty ladies in them. But one was the most beautifullest in the town. She was the most beautifullest in the whole kingdom. And the queen and king invited the most beautifullest girl in the town to their palace. Well of course they gave her a pretty bedroom too, and, of course, she had pretty dresses and she always, always had breakfast when her alarm clock rung. But she were indeed a very good one too. One day when she was sleeping she heard some galloping horses riding by. And one of them was the most handsomest one in the world. He knocked on the door. It swung open and he went in and up the winding staircase and found her lying there on the bed. Well, when she woke up she found him waiting there and they lived happily ever after. (Rachel, in Smidt 1998:165)

Each of these little stories gives evidence of the narrators having heard stories read and told. All three young story-makers believe that a story must end with everyone living happily ever after. But it seems to me – and this is purely assumption – that both Daniel and Wally have experienced more difficulties in their lives than little Rachel with her 'beautifullest' girl with her pretty dresses and a handsome prince. Daniel has written his version of a fable and includes a moral warning about not talking to strangers – known to him from the cultural messages embedded in the stories he has heard and perhaps, warnings from home. Wally, aged 5, seems to know about family disruption but also dreams of children being self-sufficient and able to cope without adults. He longs for a pet to take him away from reality. Rachel at 4 uses book language in her story, talking of the door swinging open and a winding stair-case, which suggests she has encountered a rich diet of story and fairytale.

We can also analyse these stories in terms of Bruner's categories of require-ments discussed earlier:

- The first is *agency*. Narrators must state, impute or imply some goal for the characters in the narrative. Daniel's wolf wants to play with someone; two children and the dad want to run away and Wally and Rachel 's prettiest lady wants to marry a handsome prince.
- The second is that a *sequential order* be established and maintained. This is far from well developed or sophisticated in any of the tales, although it is clear that one thing follows another fairly logically.
- The third is *not to violate the rules of narrative*, that is, the canonic structure. In all three the characters interact with one another and the language used is comprehensible to any listener.
- The last of these categories is the importance of *voice*. The voice of the narrator in each story is unique and individual.

Bruner described a small experiment done with preschool children by Joan Lucariello. The stated aim was to determine what sparked narrative activity in them. She told them a story either about a birthday party or about a child visiting a cousin of the same age. In the birthday party story there was, of course, a cake and candles to blow out. In the visit to the cousin story not much happened other than that the two children played together. Then Lucariello breached the canonic rules in both the stories. For example, in the birthday party stories she might make the girl whose birthday it was unhappy.

To be unhappy on your own birthday is unexpected. Or she ensured that some-one poured water on the candles rather than blowing them out, when every-one knows the rule is to blow birthday candles out. Likewise she breached canonicality in some of the visiting cousin tales. A visit to a cousin is much less fixed and routine than a birthday party so it is hard to predict what might happen. Therefore the breaches in these stories seemed odd, rather than a travesty of the rules.

After the story telling session the children were asked questions about what had happened in the story. The first thing Lucariello found was that the chil-dren listening to the birthday story where rules were breached gave more complex and innovative narrative accounts to explain this. One child said that the little girl whose birthday it was was unhappy because she had for-gotten about it the day before and so was not wearing a party dress. In the breach of the few canon rules in the visiting cousin stories children invented simpler explanations. But all the explanatory narratives invoked an inten-tional state: the little girl forgot her birthday, with a cultural given that on your birthday you wear a party dress.

Bruner explains that this shows children make sense of a cultural aberration by appealing to some subjective state in the character. Children understand that in their culture it is expected that the party child wear special clothes for her birthday party and a reason must be found for a child not doing so. One plausible explanation is that the child must have forgotten the exact date of her birthday. Bruner reminds us how astounding it is that 4 year olds can come to understand what is expected and make up explanations for why it has not happened.

Peggy Miller (1995) looked at young children's experience of narrative, start-ing with examining stories told primarily by mothers to children, but also those told within earshot of the children. You so often hear a mother or other carer tell a story about a funny thing a child said or did, how naughty a child had been, what happened in the house next door and other everyday hap-penings. There is an almost endless stream of stories. In this Baltimore study a story was told by a mother to a child or within the child's hearing, approxi-mately every seven minutes. Not surprisingly, many of these little narratives dealt with violence, aggression, threats, death, abuse and other disturbing aspects of life in this low income community. Miller reports how a 32 month old child, having overheard an adult story about a choking incident, later pro-duce her own version, complete with appropriate sound effects, gestures and discussion of the dangers of 'eating beer'.

## Narrative as rhetoric

Judy Dunn (1988) looked at children's social development in the context of their own homes. She saw that within the everyday drama of family life, the child was sometimes an actor, sometimes a protagonist, sometimes the agent, sometimes the victim and sometimes the accomplice. This role playing starts when the child is not yet using spoken language. Early on, what the child is making meaning of in these everyday dramas is what is allowed and what not, what leads to which outcome, who gets the blame and from whom.

At home children often hear accounts of their own actions, intentions and interactions from their parents or siblings and these are often described in terms of family politics. The child may be described as being to blame for something and it is not unusual for this to refer to a situation where the child sees herself as not to blame but as victim. So the child hears narratives that may be not neutral but biased, to place or escape blame, recruit an ally or defend a position. Each narrative is tailored to more than telling: each is told to justify what happened.

Bruner suggests that from this children are learning a form of *rhetoric*, the art of using language effectively and persuasively. Using language in this way requires negative skills – deceit, flattery and deception, for example. Whilst the child learns ways of understanding and interpreting what is heard, she also becomes more able to intuit what others feel, experience empathy and become a full partner in human culture.

It is clear that the making of a narrative involving complex cognitive skills like memory, sequence, comparison, use of words or pictures, ascribing aims and intentions, considering the feelings of others. It is how children come to be able to share their thoughts and feelings, desires and intentions, wishes and dreams, fears and passions.

## Documenting and analysing children's narratives

Much is written about children as consumers of knowledge and fantasy. In reality they are at the same time active constructors of knowledge, fantasy and culture. Stig Brostrom (2002) described the *Storyride* Project, in which about 400 schools and settings in Nordic countries invited children to tell their own stories, which were recorded. An adult then read the child's story back to the child so the child could choose to leave it as it was or revise or illustrate it.The final versions were then put into envelopes and mailed to children in a twinned setting in one of the other countries involved. At the time of writing Brostrom had tracked about 4,000 stories in total.

The project was respectful of children's agency and independence. This meant they were not asked to tell stories: instead there were times of the day or places in the setting for story making or story telling to take place collaboratively. Children's play was observed and recorded to analyse the differences and similarities between narratives told and narratives created collaboratively with peers.

The researchers define stories as being either *personal*, where they are drawn directly from lived experience and the storyteller is at the heart of the story, or *genuine*. The genuine stories must conform to the requirements below:

- have a beginning, a middle and an end
- be made up of events carried out in the past and by humans
- include actions that are intentional and given outward expression through being told or acted out with the purpose of understanding or organising aspects of the story maker's world
- contain a plot of linked and logically connected actions allowing meaning to be made from the whole thing and not just a part.

Interesting though this is, I am not persuaded that stories have to be about humans. We are familiar with the many stories children hear and invent which have animals as characters. This seems to be a perfectly acceptable form of story and allows the child more safety in expressing controversial or difficult ideas.

Brostrom cites the small narrative below, told by 5 year old Mark, as an example of a personal story, which is a re-telling of some event in the life of the story-maker:

> Somebody is fighting, this is my little sister and me. We only fight for fun. One more is fighting. This is me and this is not for fun. (Brostrom, 200:88)

This appears to be rather more than a re-telling. It suggests something missing from Brostrom's criteria – the importance of affect or feelings in the telling of the tale. Mark is telling us what he feels about fighting. Much of the analysis of the story-making in this project is very statistical and it is referenced at the end of the book for those who want to follow it up.

When children start to use narrative structure in story-making their narratives can be analysed in terms of five levels:

- A starting point where everything is normal and peaceful, as for example 'one day, when the sun was shining', or 'once upon a time there was a little girl...'

- ▨ The peace is then destroyed or a problem introduced, such as 'the father fell ill' or ''suddenly, out of the woods, came...'
- ▨ A period of chaos and turmoil follows where attempts are made to re-establish the peace or solve the problem, such as 'then the doctor arrived' or 'he ran after the creature'
- ▨ The re-establishment of the original peace begins, such as ' they followed the wolf' or 'he kissed her and she awoke'
- ▨ A new balance arises so that the problem is resolved, peace reigns and something has changed, as in 'they all lived happily ever after' or 'she married the frog' – or should that be prince?

Vygotsky called some stories *primitive* where events are linked in a rather haphazard fashion so that although there is a sequence, the relationship of one event to another may not be apparent to the reader or listener. It is important to remember that the relationship between the events may be wholly evident to the child story-maker, if not to the listener. Paley is wonderful at recognising all narratives as stories and able to get the children to expand on what they were thinking about or concerned with in the making of the story. In this way she shows that what sometimes looks random, haphazard and illogical is not, in the eyes of the child. Here is an example told by Aaron:

> 'Me and my dog are going trick or treating. We went to a spooky house that had a ghost. We ran home and my mom saved us'. (p92)

A straightforward story with a beginning, a middle and an end – and a happy one. No much happens and so on, the surface, this is a pretty ordinary little story, until you realise, as Paley did, that Aaron does not live with his mother. But he does know how he would like things to be. This serves as an important reminder that the more you know about the children in your care the better you will understand and interpret their stories.

When researchers set about analysing the themes of stories written *for* children they found the following contradiction pairs or dyads, none of which are surprising:

- ▨ power and weakness – as, for example, when little Jack defeats the Giant
- ▨ good versus wicked – where the good fairy outwits the wicked witch
- ▨ attack and defence – where the little pigs build houses to keep the wolf out
- ▨ chase and being chased – as where the gingerbread man runs and runs to escape being eaten

■ care and friendship – as where Mary in the Secret Garden makes friends with Dickon.

■ happiness and unhappiness – as in the happy ending to the Cinderella story

In their analysis of the children's stories, researchers found a marked difference between the ways in which boys and girls used these contradiction pairs. Girls focused primarily on the last two – relating to care and friendship, happiness and unhappiness, whilst boys focused on attack and defence, good versus wicked, control and power.

Children become narrators because they have developed expectations about how the world should be. They develop these expectations through their experiences, interactions, patterns and regularities in the word and the stories they have heard and read. They also enjoy the unexpected, unusual, fantastic and surprising. Their narratives often include examples where the everyday joins with the fantastic, the ordinary with the possible.

Here, to end this chapter, is a tiny narrative made by 4 year old Octavia. It illustrates perfectly how she was able to draw on what must have seemed fantastic and magical to her, the everyday wonder of an earthworm emerging in the everyday place of the garden.

> Once upon a time when I was little in my garden there were a earthworm coming out of my plant. (Smidt, 1998:165)

# 11

## Adopting and subverting the real world through narrative in role play

Beatrice:      pretend we got out when you were not looking and you didn't see
Tabitha:       and and you thought a monster had gotched us yeah?
(Martin and Dombey, 2002:54)

P lay is what children do when they follow their own interests and passions. They ask and answer questions that arise as they continually seek to make meaning, understand and explain their world. In play, which is sometimes solo but often collaborative, they explore real and imaginary worlds.

This chapter considers two aspects of story-making. The first is how children create imaginary worlds, drawn from their experience of the real world and their explorations of other possible worlds, past or future, to create their own literature. The second is how, through adopting roles drawn from the real world and their explorations of other possible worlds, they use language and negotiation to live out their stories.

### Reality and fairy tales

After the Russian Revolution it was decided that it was important for the new society to focus on reality and hence ensure that young children were not exposed to traditional or fairy tales, which are so drenched in fantasy and imagination. In 1924 a mother and paediatrician called Stanchinskaia wrote the following words in a Moscow magazine:

> We propose to replace the unrealistic folk tales and fantasies with simple realistic stories taken from the world of reality and nature. (cited in Chukovsky, 1963:119)

In the diary she kept of her own child's development she recorded what he said as he developed his own internal fantasy world. He pretended that a red elephant came to live in his room; he created an imaginary friend, a bear named Cora. So real did Cora seem to him that he would warn his mother not sit on a particular chair because Cora was sitting there. When it snowed he became a reindeer. A rug he sat on became a ship. It was clear that not having fairy or folk tales to draw on did not stop him playing in his invented worlds, peopled with characters of his own creation, and acting out anything or everything that excited, interested, challenged or scared him.

This child was subverting the real world to suit his own internal needs. It seems that the urge to narrate survives whatever the demands of the real world. Chukovsky gives many examples of the wonderful ways in which children ask and answer questions that arise from their real lives and which they answer through their play or exploration. He noted how often children adapt their responses to events in the real world to match or address their feelings and needs. Here are examples:

After hearing the story of Little Red Riding-Hood one little boy expunged the wolf from the story and gave his own very abbreviated version which goes like this:

> 'Once upon a time there was little Riding-Hood and she went and opened the door. That's all. I don't know any more of it!'
> 'And the wolf?'
> 'We don't want a wolf. I'm afraid of him.' (p45)

> Chukovsky tells of his 3 year old granddaughter playing so that her books, spread out on the floor became a river in which she caught fish or washed her clothes. When she accidentally stepped on one of the books she shouted out 'Oh, I got my foot all wet.' (p120)

> Some children were playing Sleeping Beauty; their attention was soon diverted to something else and they left the Princess sleeping on a shelf
> 'Come to dinner!' her grandmother called to her.
> 'I can't. I'm the Princess. I'm asleep.' (p121)

## The invented world of Angria

We know that many young children start sharing their stories and even recording them in some way. Possibly the best known example of early books made by children are those of Charlotte, Branwell, Emily and Anne Bronte. These four surviving Bronte children, living with their father in the parsonage in Haworth, spent much of their time playing and their play allowed them to act out their real life traumas (the loss of their mother and subsequently two sisters) and the events of their everyday and imagined lives. From all this they began to construct and play out stories, individually and collaboratively.

The three girls had little formal schooling whereas their brother, Branwell, was sent off to school. There were books and poems in their home and they had access to two Leeds newspapers and to *Blackwoods Magazine*, a conservative journal offering work by Shelley and Coleridge, and recognised as being a powerful influence on the work of Charles Dickens and Edgar Allan Poe. Deeply important and influential in their lives were the moors where they lived and which were to feature so strongly in Emily's single tragic novel, the fantastic and romantic *Wuthering Heights.*

As the children read and played they began to write down their stories. They did so in minute books. The spelling was poor, there was little in the way of punctuation and their work was modelled on the styles of writing they had encountered. The tiny handwriting seems to have been designed to keep adults at bay. Consequently no one commented on their handwriting, spelling or punctuation or other surface features of their work. As they became more experienced readers, they became more skilled and accurate composers and rather better at spelling. Their imaginations were free to flourish. It is worth taking account of this in light of some of the things people working with young children pay attention to and comment on when responding to children's writing.

Juliet Barker (2010), who has written about the Bronte's childhood, described how we find in their writing battles and rebellions, accounts of political events, characters based on famous people, early attempts at satire and humour and the creation of whole shared worlds.

Words attributed to Charlotte describe how some of the writing came about:

> Papa bought Branwell some wooden soldiers at Leeds; when Papa came home it was night, and we were in bed, so next morning Branwell came to our door with a box of soldiers. Emily and I jumped out of bed, and I snatched up one and exclaimed, 'This is the Duke of Wellington! This shall be the Duke!' When I had said this Emily likewise took one up and said it should be hers; when Anne came down, she said one should be hers. Mine was the prettiest of the whole, and the tallest, and the most perfect in every part. Emily's was a grave-looking fellow, and we called him 'Gravey.' Anne's was a queer little thing, much like herself, and we called him 'Waiting-boy.' Branwell chose his, and called him 'Bonaparte.'

(Charlotte Brontë's 'History of the Year 1829' as published by Elizabeth Gaskell, *The Life of Charlotte Brontë* (http://www.lang.nagoya-u.ac.jp/~matsuoka/EG-Charlotte-1.html#V)

This makes clear how the children used objects at hand to be characters in their invented worlds, much as Hannah did with the toy plastic dinosaurs. It also shows how the identities of their created characters were determined by who they resembled or what they reminded the children of.

Subsequently the Bronte children created an imaginary country on the west coast of Africa, which they originally called Glasstown but later renamed Angria. In this country were real places like the Niger River but also cities that were entirely fictitious, such as Verdopilis. They peopled the country with various characters who were placed in homes and places drawn from Yorkshire culture and what they had read in books or newspapers. Sometimes they merged imaginary and real worlds so that in one story we may find an imaginary happening alongside a comment about a political event in their real lives. As the children became older their writing changed to include irony; reflections on drunkenness, which they had witnessed at first hand because of Branwell's alcoholism; considerations of loneliness; thoughts on the role of women; reflections on the importance of learning, together with a broad knowledge of classical literature and borrowings from the works of real and published authors. Thus there is a complex weaving of making sense of life, together and collaboratively, as well as alone and privately.

Charlotte, Emily and Anne all went on to become published authors only by pretending to be men. Tragic Branwell, cherished and only son, became addicted to opium and alcohol and died young. Some of his poetry was published. What is interesting is how the Bronte siblings used narrative, written, spoken and acted out, with determination and focus, as the driving force which allowed them to change their lives. Howe (2001) argues that their genius – in fact, all genius – is not a gift but is achieved through a combination of influences, environment, personality and perseverance.

## Active engagement or passive consumption: the power of theatre

The work of thinkers like Piaget, Vygotsky and Bruner has shown that, from birth, children work incredibly hard to make sense of this world they inhabit. They are by nature active rather than passive; agents rather than mere consumers. We see this particularly clearly when children are fortunate enough to be taken to the theatre. What they encounter there is often complex and sometimes multilayered. Children are experienced at reading images and playing roles. They have also watched others in the real world behaving 'as if' and of doing that themselves in their role play. They construct narratives in which they make connections between the familiar and the strange at the same time and through their experience of narratives heard and seen and read they know how to step right into someone else's imaged world.

The more fortunate have already done this through exposure to wordless picturebooks. But the theatre offers added dimensions. There is the the use of lights to emphasise, hide, distort or change; the use of music or sound effects to accompany or distract from or add to the narrative. And there is the wonderful way in which more than one narrative can be unveiled at the same time. Children, apart from and yet drawn into what is happening, have to suspend disbelief and learn to trust those making the narrative in front of their very eyes.

I took some children who were not experienced theatre-goers to the Unicorn Theatre and when one of the characters asked the audience to look up and see the sky and I did, one of the children asked me why I had looked up when I must have known that above us was not the sky but the ceiling of the theatre. I was saddened that this literal-minded child was reluctant to let go of reality and enter the world of the possible.

Taking children to the theatre can be a magical experience for adults as they watch the children being drawn into what is happening in front of them make links with their own experience as they enter a world created by someone they don't know. If, as Bruner said, the engine of narrative is trouble (1996), what better way to encounter it than through the unfolding layers of narrative being acted out before your eyes. Here is an imagined world where the story is exposed scene by scene rather than page by page. In each scene more than one thing can be happening and the viewer can see the story unfolding through different perspectives all happening at the same time. Child viewers can see adults and other children taking on the roles of invented people or creatures, encountering trouble in differing forms, overcoming or learning to live with the consequences of this, negotiating, collaborating and sometimes stepping into and out of roles, just as they do in their own pretend play. The sadness is that many children do not have the opportunity to experience that magic moment when the theatre darkens and the audience sits there waiting to see what will happen.

Philip Pullman says that 'the audience in the dark are makers too.' He is talking not only of the physical dark but also of the unknown. The at-first unknowing children must make meaning from what unfolds before their eyes. They are co-constructors of the narrative.

An awareness is growing of the power of theatre to help children move beyond the current nature of objective-driven educational experiences to thinking and feeling for themselves. Theatres for children, like new books for children, address real and deep issues, as well as offering delightful escapism. At the Unicorn Theatre and others, children are invited to step into a world where they explore the real lives of street children or have to work out who to trust, think about their own rights as children, clap their hands to stop Tinkerbell from dying, weep for the death of a wounded horse or shudder at the sight of demons. In other words they are offered opportunities to be reflective about moral, troubling and painful issues as well as celebrate more joyous events.

There are dedicated children's theatres in many places in the world. London boasts the Unicorn, Little Angel Puppet Theatre, Polka Theatre and more. Plays designed for children and their parents also offered at the National Theatre, which is where Philip Pullman's *His Dark Materials* and Michael Morpurgo's *War Horse* were first performed. There are permanent children's theatres throughout Europe – The Ark in Dublin, La Montagne Magique in Brussels, Het Palais in Antwerp and Unga Klara in Stockholm. In 2006/7 there was a wonderful collaboration, celebrating children's literature and theatre, between the Swedish government and the Unicorn Theatre.

## A topsy-turvy world in play

Watch and listen to young children engaged in role play and you will see and hear yourself, authority figures, characters drawn from stories, adult phrases, different tones of voice and styles of body language. As young children select and adopt roles to play they not only mimic but exaggerate and create in order to dramatise and highlight features of notions such as authority. Teachers may adopt a particular stance, use an identifiable way of speaking or praise or punish children. Yet again we see children not merely imitating but transforming. So, as they explore dramatic conflict, domestic bliss or everyday life in the classroom or setting or imaged adventures in the forest or castle, they subvert reality. Chukovsky said that, in doing this, they were with delight creating a topsy-turvy world. Bruner showed how important games involving prediction and surprise are for young children, who pay particular attention when something strange or unexpected occurs. They then use this in their narratives. Something strange, surprising or unexpected is turning the world upside down, subverting it. Garvey (1977) suggested that as soon as a child has learned how things ought to be, she turns them upside down or distorts them in some way, just for the fun of seeing what will happen. So the child becoming the teacher is fiercer and stricter than any real teacher; the magic spell she casts is more powerful than any spell ever cast before and her medical skills allow her to bring her patient back to life. Note the language used by the speakers in the roles adopted by them in the examples below:

- Lee is being the teacher and phones Cathy, playing the role of mother of a pupil. Lee says 'Hello Miss Rhodes? ... Your daughter's gone on a trip and she won't be back until about six o'clock tomorrow night ... I imagine she stayed overnight at school so I'm very sorry about that.' (Williams, 2004:60)

- Madison goes into the dramatic play area and tells Anne that she is a boy. Madison then spends a long time making her room out of blocks and says over and over again 'I am a boy and I am building my own bed'. When Anne later offers her some jewellery as a present she reacts violently and says 'Yuck! ... I'm not a girl. I am not a girl! These are girl things and I don't wear them.' (Blaise, 2005:147)

- The third example refers to Daniella, examining the sick baby in the home corner. She says 'She is very sick. Put her there ... and take her hat off. Her eyes are flashing and her ears are sore.' She puts a spoon in the doll's ear and makes the noise 'sloosh,sloosh' and says 'Now, that's better.' (Smidt, 2010:44)

Lee, as teacher, uses very formal language which he might not use unless in role. You see this particularly in the sentence 'I imagine she stayed overnight at school'. Madison, who really hates being a girl, adopts the role of being a boy with zest and furiously keeps insisting that she is not a girl and rejecting what she sees as things for girls. Daniella as mother, nurse, carer or doctor uses wonderfully descriptive language to describe the baby's illness and clearly knows about prescribing and giving medicines. Both her parents are doctors.

### In role or out of role?

It has been traditional to analyse the behaviour and language used by children in their chosen roles in terms of how well they are able to mimic the role of the person they are playing. So, for example, we could expect Lee as teacher to have some understanding of just how teachers speak and possibly act, and of the types of gesture and expression they use. We have seen some of this in the three little examples earlier in this chapter. But there are more dynamic processes at work and Martin and Dombey (2002) suggest that the distinctions between being in and out of role, of being in play or not, are not so sharply defined. In play children may well turn things upside down and inside out but they usually do so to explore their own concerns and feelings. We see that with Madison and her dissatisfaction with her lot as a girl.

Children do this not only in their play but in their narratives, which they construct according to their concerns and feelings. Consider Wally's narratives discussed earlier. He created a family made of a man and a mother, two sisters and a brother. Then the adults ran away one after the other until only the youngest were left. Magically they acquired a lion as a pet and having always wanted a pet they lived happily ever after. It seems that Wally is drawing on his own unhappy family experience, together with his knowledge of stories and possible worlds to deal with his fears and feelings.

Amy Paugh carried out an interesting study where she looked at how children in Dominica in the Caribbean became involved in code-switching in their role play. There is some literature about how children choose the style of language they use in their role play to indicate the status, class and role of the person they are playing. There is also documentation of how children in some cultures overlay their role play with adult storytelling genres.

In two studies on bilingualism Kwan-Terry (1992), looking at Cantonese speakers, and Halmari and Smith (1994), looking at Finnish speakers, found that children used English, their second language in both cases, for imaginary characters and their first language for the *running commentary on the play or for negotiating playscripts and play frames*. This area of study looks at language socialisation and examines how children, through their interactions with more knowledgeable members of a community or more expert others, come to learn and be socialised into the cultural and linguistic knowledge which allows them to participate in everyday activities. Researchers in this field engage in detailed and subtle considerations of aspects of power, class, status, race, ethnicity, gender, morality and language itself. A well-known and often-used clip made by the Open University years ago, shows a little girl in the domestic play area playing the role of manager of a shop. Everything about her play says 'manager': the way she talks, her gestures, her body language. How does this child, not yet 5 years old, know what style of language a manager uses, what tone of voice she adopts, what gestures she makes? Has she noticed how the headteacher, perhaps, or someone she has encountered in her community, behaves and extrapolated from that just what makes someone sound and look as though they are in charge? This is a remarkable cognitive achievement, involving minute inspection, detailed analysis and extrapolation.

Play with others is a wonderful context for the use of language and cultural learning and socialisation. We have all seen children playing roles and sometimes recognise ourselves or our colleagues in their play. We know that children's play is never mere copying or mimicry but is always dynamic and creative. Any role a child plays, together with the language choices she makes, is unique. Paugh's study is interesting and can be downloaded at http://www.jmu.edu/socanth/anth/wm_library/Paugh_2005_Multilingual_Play.pdf. This is a summary of the findings – they are pretty amazing.

Paugh's research built on an earlier study by Ochs (1996), which showed that children in Dominica, like all children, engage in complex code-switching between languages in their role play, in this case between English and Patwa. The children tended to use the language most suited to the roles they were playing. Paugh set out to find what language socialisation took place through role play.

The official language of Dominica is English while Patwa is the spoken language of the rural population. Patwa is regarded with disdain by those in power, who describe it as an impoverished and oral language, whereas English represents authority, power, education and status. As children learn to speak they learn much about the languages, who uses them, for what purposes, where and when.

The majority of Dominican children acquire English as their first language now, but use Patwa for their own purposes, especially with peers. Code switching into Patwa is used to assert dominance during play and other peer situations. It is particularly noticeable in role play. In other types of play it appears that the children speak primarily in English with only occasional code-switches into Patwa.

Role playing is a common activity in the villages, where there are few bought toys. The play is infused with talk which sustains it, as the children discuss who will do what and where, what is going to happen and why, and how the play will develop. The researchers found that children used proportionately more Patwa in this play than in other activities. They also noticed differences between the children's negotiations about role play and the language used within it.

It is fascinating that although the children are not allowed to speak Patwa either at home or at school, it is the language of choice in their playscripts, settings and roles. It seems that play – particularly pretend play – offers a safe space in which they can try out language varieties and social identities without fear of adult restrictions. Although these children would use English for any situation involving power and authority in their everyday lives, here they don't. They grab hold of the opportunity to use Patwa to explore what they can do with it. They use Patwa in whichever role they have chosen to achieve any goal they have set themselves. They do not, in this safe space, use Patwa to portray submissive or lower roles. They use the language itself – Patwa – to become the leaders of play activities and hence direct and shape what their peers do. This suggests how brilliant children are at making meaning and subverting aspects of their worlds so they can challenge some of what they have understood.

When you pay careful attention to what children say and do in their role play you will notice them moving in and out of roles and will see that there is often the issue of power in this play. Some roles offer more power than others and are consequently more desirable. There are many examples of children arguing who is to be the mum, the dad, the bad guy, or the superhero. Often the child playing a particular role is perceived as being more important or powerful: in a sense the nature of the character being played transfers itself to the player. Moreover when children opt to role play together they have to work hard to create a playscript which meets the needs of all the potential players and this requires considerable skills of negotiation.

Learning to negotiate is difficult. Even adults find it so. What some skilled educators do is create opportunities for young children where if they are to carry out something that matters to them, they need to be able to collaborate, listen, discuss, argue, suggest and negotiate. One of the people who is best at doing this is Vivian Gussin Paley.

### The almost last word goes to ... Wally and his friends
Vivian Gussin Paley watches, listens, thinks, watches, listens, thinks and records. In this way she has built up an amazing collection of things children think and say, often based on their experiences of story and narrative. Her books give a real sense of this and I almost end this book with the words and ideas of Wally and his friends.

Recognising the importance of narrative in children's analysis of their world, Paley started helping them create their own narratives and work together in collaboration to act these out. She says that she helped them create a 'theatre in the round' in the classroom space and there they dramatise and act out stories based on picture-story books, fairy tales and their own narratives. The children found that picturebooks were easy to remember and understand and flexible enough to allow them to use those as the foundation for their own thoughts and ideas. By contrast, fairy tales allowed children to re-enact and re-experience more serious themes in greater depth.

To give you a flavour of how some of this work went here is a short extract from when the children were re-enacting the fairy tale *The Tinder-Box*. This is the story of a soldier who returns from the wars, does a favour for a witch and consequently becomes very wealthy. The soldier carries out brutal acts like cutting off heads, but in the end he marries the princess and, of course, lives happily ever after. Paley asked the children why the soldier had had to cut off the witch's head, why he had to kill her. Lisa said that it was so she could not change him into a frog. Wally added that it was so she could not change him into a rock. Fred insisted that it did not matter because witches can't be dead because they know magic. Here is a little of the discussion that followed:

| | |
|---|---|
| Teacher: | ...why didn't she come alive and get back her tinder box? |
| Eddie: | It's one of the hardest things to do. It takes about a hundred weeks to do that. |
| Deana: | Why didn't the witch go down herself to get the tinder box? |
| Jill: | Then who would pull her up? |
| Warren: | Why didn't she get a ladder? |
| Jill: | Maybe she didn't even have a ladder. |
| Eddie: | A magic person can make a ladder appear. |
| Warren: | Witches have brooms |
| Wally: | The soldier could hold her up |

(Paley, 1981:67-8)

These children are 5 years old. How hard they are working to make sense of this story and how well they are listening to one another and building on one another's contributions. Eddie has a theory about why the witch can't come back to life and sees that the difficulty of this can be expressed in terms of a very, very long time. Deana follows up with a suggestion of a more simple action. Jill then realises that the witch could not act alone. Warren has a solution to that – a ladder. He also knows that witches may not be able to magic up ladders since they only have brooms.

Here is the same group of children, now trying to resolve the difficulty of how to measure two rugs they want to use in their re-enactment of *Jack and the Beanstalk*. Observe the enormous amount of mathematical thinking going on. Wally and Eddie disagree about whether the two rugs are the same size or not:

| | |
|---|---|
| Wally: | The big rug is the giant's castle. The small one is Jack's house. |
| Eddie: | Both rugs are the same. |

| Wally: | They can't be the same. Watch me. I'll walk round the rug. Now watch – walk, walk, walk, walk, walk, walk, walk, walk, walk – count all these walks. Now count the other rug. Walk, walk, walk, walk, walk. See? That one has more walks. |
| --- | --- |
| Eddie: | No fair. You cheated. You walked faster. |
| Wally: | I don't have to walk. I can just look. |
| Eddie: | I can look too. But you have to measure it. You need a ruler. About six hundred inches or feet. |
| Wally: | We have a ruler |
| Eddie: | Not that one. Not the short kind. You have to use the long kind that gets curled up in a box. |
| Wally: | Use people. People's bodies. Lying down in a row. |
| Wally.: | That's a great idea. I never even thought of that. |

(Paley, 1981:13-14)

I love this conversation. How serious the boys are and how carefully they listen to one another. It is a real and equal dialogue. They respect one another's ideas and build on them and when Wally comes up with the brainwave Eddie is so gracious in his recognition of its brilliance. What Paley does is to pay attention, show respect for and support the children in their imagined worlds, sometimes offering them anchor points to what we might regard as reality.

You, the adults involved with young children, with belief in yourself and what you value, can create a curriculum which is respectful of the ideas, needs, interests, fears, relationships and passions of the children. Literature provides you with many starting points.

## And so they lived happily ever after ... the end

This is the way good stories end. The happy ending wraps things up so that anything bad that has happened during the tale is dealt with and the child is left feeling satisfied that all has ended well. But not all endings are happy, not all stories are easy to listen to or make. Children make narratives and stories to understand what they encounter and to explain it to themselves and to others. How cognitively challenging this is! So when I urge that we really need to embed literature into the curriculum, ensuring that we share books and narratives and stories with the children and offer them multiple opportunities to make, read, illustrate and even act out their own narratives, we know that this is about more than pleasure. Although pleasure there certainly is.

I return to Chukovsky: this great Russian thinker, storyteller, linguist and psychologist devised a set of what he called 'commandments' for those making books or stories for children. They offer suggestions about the features of children's literature to look out for – a recipe to help in the selection of what to read and what to tell and how to do it. Here is my interpretation of what he said:

- The thinking of those writing for children must be *graphic* so that every word or phrase invites children to make their own images.

- The thinking must be *lyrical* so authors need to be 'poet-authors and poet singers'. Rhythm and lilt and emphasis must be built into the text. The books must be intensely *musical* to make them memorable.

- *Rhyme* and line should have pace and pulse of their own.

- Avoid *too many adjectives* so as to allow an emphasis on verbs. This complies with Chukovsky's view of children as essentially active seekers of meaning.

- Recognise and exploit the potential in books for *play and games*. These carry with them notions of rules, collaboration, negotiation, choice, give and take, and risk. It also allows for the imagined, the possible, the fantasic, the strange, the odd, the bizarre alongside the true, the actual, the visible and the seen.

- Finally, Chukovsky says that we need to bring children into what he calls adult perceptions, which I take to mean that we need to choose and make and share stories that are *about real and important things.*

The role of any educator is a complex one but it can change lives. Heinrich Mann said that 'a house without books is like a room without windows'.

We might ask if a place of learning with no books and stories is like a room without a door to open to the worlds beyond.

# Building your collection

This section provides details of the books mentioned in the text as well as other books which offer something special. They are set out, in alphabetical order chapter by chapter, with some annotations. They indicate some – and only some – of the many wonderful resources you may find useful in building your own or your school/setting's collection. If you like a book or collection mentioned look also at other work by that author.

The publication date of the edition cited is given after the title of the book but this may not be the date of first publication.

## Poetry and songs
John AGARD and Kevin DEAN *Grandfather's Old Bruk-a-down Car* (1997) Red Fox poetry

Hilaire BELLOC with Quentin BLAKE *Cautionary Verses* (2004) Red Fox poetry books

Edward LEAR *The Complete Nonsense and Other Verse* (2002) Penguin Classics

Spike MILLIGAN *Silly Verse for Kids* (1973) Puffin Book

Michael ROSEN *Quick, Let's Get Out of Here* (2007) Puffin Books; *Mustard, Custard, Grumble Belly and Gravy* (2007) Bloomsbury Paperback; *Michael's Rosen's Book of Very Silly Poems* (2007) Puffin Books

WEBB, K and MAITLAND, A (eds) *I Like This Poem: A Collection of Best-loved Poems Chosen by Children for other Children in Aid of the International Year of the Child* (2007) Puffin Books

## Folk tales, fables, nursery rhymes, fairy tales, nursery tales and others to help you learn to become a storyteller.
BROTHERS GRIMM *Six Fairy Tales* (1970) with original etchings by David Hockney. Petersburg Press.

A tiny gem of a book full of dark tales, some famous (Rapunzel and Rumpelstilzchen) and some not (Fundevogel and Old Rinkrank)

C. DOWNING *Tales of the Hodja* (1964) Oxford University Press.

A series of stories about the adventures and sayings of the Hodja, especially told for children and in this case, selected to celebrate the language and culture of a child in the class.

J. GRIMM and W. GRIMM illustrated by Mervyn PEAKE *Grimm's Household Tales* (2012) The British Library Publishing division.

Short, dark and often odd stories like The Goose Girl or The Nose Tree or the Seven Ravens.

Virginia HAMILTON and Leo and Diane DILLON (illustrators) The People Could Fly (1986) Walker Books.

A worthy book of stories from her own black ancestry heard by the writer, rooted in the slave culture. You will find trickster tales of Bruh Rabbit, outwitting larger and stronger animals; stories to laugh at; spine-chilling ghost stories and dramatic tales of freedom and escape. Powerful monochrome illustrations. The book is a useful resource although you may find yourself reading rather than telling the stories because you may feel you can't match the lilt of the language.

Kathleen LINES and Alan HOWARD (illustrator) *The Faber Storybook* (1961) Faber and Faber.

This is a well known collection and includes nonsense stories, animal folktales from many countries, traditional fairy tales involving kings and queens, and giants and witches; myths and legends, fables and stories from many sources. Includes works by the brothers Grimm, poet Walter de la Mare, Oscar Wilde, Wanda Gag. A useful resource learning some stories to tell by heart. Simple line drawings.

Kathleen LINES and Alan HOWARD (illustrator) *Lavender's Blue: A Book of Nursery Rhymes* (2004) Oxford University Press

Jacqueline Wilson chose this collection as the gift she would like to give a small child. She says of the illustrations that Jones uses a wonderful palette of delicate blue, sage green, lilac and apricot to create his own fantasy world.

Alison LURIE and Jessica SOUHAMI (illustrator) *Baba Yaga and the Stolen Baby* (2007) Frances Lincoln.

Beautifully illustrated Russian folk tale about the witch Baba Yaga and the forgetful child, Elena. There are more in a similar style and they are worth collecting. See under Souhami in this section.

Robert MCDOWELL and Edward LAVITT and Barbara Kohn ISAAC (illustrator) *Third World Voices for Children* (1973) Allison and Busby Ltd.

An old collection of stories with black and white line drawings, legends, poems and songs from Africa, the Caribbean, the United States and Papua-New Guinea. Includes some fine creation myths.

Geraldine MCCAUGHREAN *The Orchard Book of Greek Myths* (1992) Orchard.

Sixteen favourite Greek myths adapted by a talented storyteller with illustrations by Emma Chichester Clark. Series includes *The Orchard Book of Roman Myths* (2003)

Sir Sherlock Philip MANDERSON and Gioia FIAMMENGHI I *The Iguana's Tail: Crick Crack Stories from the Caribbean* (1977) Andre Deutsch.

A collection of animal stories from the Caribbean re-told and easy enough to recall to allow new storytellers to build their confidence.

N. NYEMBE *Children's Stories from Africa* (2004) Monterey Video

This DVD offers two sets of fables and songs from African cultures. It celebrates storytelling but it needs to be used carefully, ideally as a tool for you as prospective storyteller, rather than for the children as audience. It falls into the trap of exoticising the images.

Iona and Peter OPIE *The Lore and Language of Schoolchildren* (1959) New York Review of Books.

A famous and invaluable collection of playground rhymes.

Jessica SOUHAMI *King Pom and the Fox* (2009) Frances Lincoln.

Chinese version of Puss-in-Boots with a fox instead of a cat.

Jessica SOUHAMI *The Leopard's Drum – an Asante Tale from West Africa* (1996) Frances Lincoln.

Delightful illustrations based on Souhami's beautiful shadow puppets. Available in dual text English/Bengali and English /Punjabi. Look out for more of her books

Hugh TRACEY and E. BYRD (illustrations) and A.TRACEY (music) *The Lion on the Path and other African stories* (1967) Routledge and Kegan Paul.

I love this collection of traditional stories from Southern Africa. Translated into English, they feature animals in roles many children can identify with. Python the healer, Rabbit the trickster, Tortoise the wise. Some stories have songs with musical notation, black and white line drawings, lots of repetition and dialogue. Wonderful material for telling – all you need is confidence and a good memory!

## Websites

http://www.pitt.edu/-dash/folktexts.html offers details and examples of a vast range of folk and fairy tales, myths and legends, sagas and others, edited and/or translated by D.L.Ashliman of the University of Pittsburgh.

http://www.xanthegresham.co.uk is the website of a performance story teller who will do storytelling sessions and workshops with children. Go to her website to find out more. She is the storyteller for Tate Britain

## Picturebooks without words

Use these books with care, ideally with only one or two children or with small groups so the child is in control of making the narrative from the pictures. You may be surprised by how sophisticated many of these books are and how much they offer to older children. Look at them before you offer them.

Allan and Janet AHLBERG *The Baby's Catalogue* (2010) Puffin

A book of baby things and a naming book rather than a narrative. All their books are worth looking at but remember that they represent an idealised notion of childhood which is not always appropriate.

Mitsumas ANNO *Anno's Journey* (2005) Putnam Publishing Group, US.

A well loved picturebook with plots and sub-plots, characters and minor characters. The characters make a main journey and other subsidiary journeys through places and seasons and people.

Keith BAKER *Hide and Snake* (1995) Harcourt Children's Books.

Baker's books are interesting and require the child to interact with them so they become like games. If difficult to find in bookshops, order them online. Try amazon.com (the US version) rather than amazon.co.uk

Raymond BRIGGS *The Snowman* (2009) Puffin.

James builds a snowman in the garden and wakes up in the night to find that the snowman has come to life. James takes him into his house and in return the snowman takes him on a magical journey. A classic.

Pat HUTCHINS *Rosie's Walk* (2009) Red Fox Picture Books.

Rosie the hen goes for a walk around the farmyard pursued by the hungry but clumsy fox. One disaster after another befalls the fox whilst Rosie continues, completely oblivious. Colourful, humorous and almost wordless.

Suzy LEE is an up and coming book maker who constructs books which are art in their own right. She is one of the featured authors in the book. Her books include:

*Wave* (2008) Chronicle books.

The simple tale of a small girl's day at the beach.The narrative is carried by the pictures alone and each detail adds to the possible narratives being made by the observer.

*Shadow* (2010) Chronicle Books.

Lee plays with the format and layout of the book, allowing the narrative to be made according to the orientation of the picture. A little girl plays in the attic with found objects and their shadows come to life. The developing narrative allows the child to consider aspects of reality and fantasy, safety and fear.

Barbara LEHMAN *The Red Book* (2004) Houghton Mifflin Harcourt.

This book won several awards. It tells of a young girl on the streets of New York finding a book and through it being transported on a magical journey. Although written for young children it is surprisingly complex and may need to be used with care. Lehman's many wordless books include *Museum Trip* (2006).

Jan ORMEROD *Moonlight* (2005) Frances Lincoln and (2005) *Sunshine* Frances Lincoln.

Classic books about the rituals of the day, both republished in 2005 but may be too culture specific to interest all children

Shaun TAN *The Red Tree* (2010) Hodder Children's Books.

A little girl wakes up feeling as though there is nothing to look forward to but then a little red seedling changes everything. This Australian artist has produced a visual fable, a book about feelings and about how people sometimes feel sad but there is always hope. Tan's book called *The Arrival* (2007) is a wordless graphic novel which tells the story of every refugee. It is very dark and and invites the beholder to raise many questions. The illustrations are remarkable and allow children to create their own stories. Suitable for older or mature younger children.

L. WARD *The Silver Pony: a story in pictures.* (1992) Houghton Mifflin.

A complex wordless story. With prompting and support young, children can create a narrative. Features a strong and bold girl, loved and adventurous.

## Picturebooks: the story is illustrated or the illustrations carry a parallel story

Verna AARDEMA and Leo and Diane DILLON *Why Mosquitoes Buzz* (1978) Pied Piper Books.

Verna AARDEMA and Beatriz VIDAL (illustrator) *Bringing the Rain to Kapiti Plain* (1986) Picturemacs.

Both books feature colourful illustrations and text with repeated refrains which are easy for children to join in with and remember.

Allan and Janet AHLBERG have written and illustrated many wonderful picturebooks for young children reminding them of previous experience but very rooted in English middle class culture. They are published by Puffin Books and include:

*Each, Peach, Pear, Plum* (1989) and *Peepo* (2004)

which refer back not only to experience but also to other texts, specifically songs and rhymes.

*The Jolly Postman* (2010)

an extremely cleverly constructed book playing with aspects of text and written materials.

*Burglar Bill* (2004)

with a working class villain as hero

*Starting School* (2011)

which shows a range of children from different cultures all sharing the experience of starting school.

ATINUKE *Anna Hibiscus* (2007) Walker Books.

Written by a Nigerian storyteller about a child's life and everyday adventures in her African home, the first in a series of books.

S. BARTRAM *Man on the Moon: A Day in the Life of Bob* (2005) Templar Publishing.

This book and CD tells the story of Bob who works on the moon as a moon expert and knows for certain that there is no such thing as an alien, whilst the pictures tell a different version, as aliens appear throughout, stealing his cake at a picnic, on the bus and even in his bath. These last two books are discussed in the chapter on translation.

F. BENJAMIN and M. CHAMBERLAIN (illustrator) *My Two Grannies* (2009) Francis Lincoln.

This book tells the story of a child who has a granny from Trinidad and one from the north of England. It is a worthy book with charming pictures but falls into the trap of glossing over serious issues. The characters are sadly two dimensional.

Eileen BROWN *Hamda's Hen* (2003) and *Hamda's Surprise* (2006) Walker Books.

These are especially popular books, with bright illustrations and cumulative texts.

Anthony BROWNE is a featured author who is referred to throughout this book. His books, published by Walker Books, are intricate and multi-layered books and include:

*Into the Forest* (2005)

One night a boy wakes up hearing a terrible sound. There is a storm. Dad has gone and mum does not know when he will be back. She warns him not to go into the forest, but he ignores her, goes into the forest and learns the fate of his father.

Hansel and Gretel (2008)

The traditional story transformed by Browne's multilayered and dark illustration.

*The Shape Game* (2004), *Voices in the Park* (1999), *Gorilla* (2008), *My Dad* (2003), *My Mum* (2008), *Piggybook* (2008)

are among Browne's remarkable, unique, funny, tragic, disturbing and intricate books and warrant great attention.

Eve BUNTING and David DIAZ (illustrator) (1999) *Smoky Night* Thomson Learning 1st Voyager Books.

A picturebook telling the story of a child in an inner city area in the United States who hears the frightening sounds of a riot outside the window. There is a fire and a rescue and a happy ending. It features a black family and the illustrations are detailed and unusual. But check before reading it aloud because very young children may be frightened by it.

**John BURNINGHAM** is a great author/artist and all his books are worth looking at. Published by Red Fox.

*Mr Gumpy's Outing* (2001)

is a book mentioned in my text. It is the story of an adventure on a boat and the antics of the animals. Wonderful use of language which is subtly didactic.

*Would You Rather?* (1994)

is a book to make children laugh as they have to choose between strange and sometimes disgusting things – whether to eat spider stew, slug dumplings, mashed worms or drink snail squash.

*Grandpa* (2003)

is about the bond between a little girl and her grandfather. Both narrative and illustrations are extremely sensitive. It has made children – and even their teachers – cry!

*Come Away from the Water, Shirley* (1992)

brilliantly illustrates parallel stories where text and illustrations may or may not tell the same story, and this applies also to *Where's Julius?* (2001)

*Oi! Get Off Our Train* (1991)

This wonderfully entitled book about the environment, how it is changing and what this might mean, all embedded in a fabulous tale with brilliant images.

*The Shopping Basket* (1992)

by contrast, is the delightfully funny everyday story of a little boy going shopping with his mental shopping list.

### Rod CAMPBELL *Dear Zoo* (1985) Picture Puffin

This is a carefully thought out board book, also available in paperback, where the reader must lift the flaps to see what is inside. The text is simple and repetitive. It is based on the peekaboo or hide and reveal games which Bruner called formats. Ideal for babies and very young children

**Nicola CAMPBELL and Kim LAFAVE** (illustrator) *Shi-shi-etko* (2010) and *Shin-Chi's Canoe* (2008) Groundwood Books.

These attractively illustrated small books from Canada reflect the traumas experienced by some aboriginal children who have to attend boarding schools. In essence they explore what it is like to lose one's culture.

**Eric CARLE** is a well known author whose work remains popular with children, their parents and toy makers. Published by Puffin Books, they include:

*The Very Hungry Caterpillar* (1997)

A classic, the story traces the life cycle of the caterpillar, charting everything he eats throughout the days of the week. It is a straightforward and brilliantly illustrated book that is also a game. The book is available in a range of sizes and formats, with accompanying puppets and other toys. Very suitable for young children and babies – and their parents, carers and educators!

*Brown Bear, Brown Bear, What Do You See?* (1997)

This is another classic with gorgeous tissue-paper collage illustration and rhyming text. There is no real narrative until the end of the story, which comes as a surprise. Carle 'teaches' colours through this book just as he teaches the names of foods and the days of the week in *The Very Hungry Caterpillar*, but the teaching is skillfully hidden in the context.

Trish COOKE and Helen OXENBURY (illustrator) *So Much!* (2008) Walker Books.

The wonderful tale of an extended African-Caribbean family loving the new baby. Cooke uses many linguistic devices to create suspense and invite prediction, as people arrive to welcome and cuddle the baby

Trish COOKE and Paul HOWARD (illustrator) *Full, Full, Full of Love* (2004) Walker Books.

Jay Jay and all his extended family always have Sunday dinner at Grannies and what a lot of good and love there is to share. Cooke has created another book about family love.

Alexis DEACON *Beegu* (2004) His books are published by Red Fox

An enchanting book about how Beegu is ignored, overlooked and rejected by the adults as he is stranded on earth. The illustrations in a limited palette show an ankle-high view some of them have of the world.

*While You Are Sleeping* (2007)

This is a very reassuring story. While a little girl sleeps, her toys tuck her in, check for monsters, make sure she does not get cold, and care for her.

Tomie DE PAOLO *Pancakes for Breakfast* (1990) Voyager Books.

A little old lady tries to make pancakes for her breakfast. A kitchen story full of recognisable objects, ingredients, humour and optimism.

Julia DONALDSON and Axel SCHEFFLER *The Gruffalo* (2010) Macmillan Books.

This new children's classic has a wonderful rhyming text that almost flies off the page and into the child's imagination. A fairly traditional adventure tale dealing with the fear of being lost or abandoned or encountering fearful things. You can get *The Gruffalo* toys, wall calendars, year planners, towels, face cloths and more!

Other of their books include *Room on the broom* (2002) *The snail and the whale* (2004) and more.

Lissa EVANS and John LIGHT *The Flower* (2006) Child's Play Library.

A beautifully illustrated book using limited colour as it explores a complex text about a boy on a mission to restore the 'soul' to the earth. Though the story is sophisticated the pictures offer endless opportunities for reflection and discussion. But becoming hard to find.

EVANS has written another book, *Small Change for Stuart*, due to be published by Corgi Children's in May 2012 and shortlisted for the Costa Prize. It is an adventure story about a 10 year old boy who has to move house, where he encounters dreadful neighbours and goes in search of a lost workshop. On his journey he finds clues to follow, puzzles to work out, danger to overcome and the need to work with others.

Sarah FANELLI *Dear Diary* (2001) Walker Books.

A fictional diary made by a highly regarded picturebook artist. Seven different diaries in the book each tell the events of one busy day.

Try also *My Map Book* (1995)

which is effectively a picture of book with maps of different things including my family, my day and my tummy.

Or *Wolf (1997)*

which is the fantastically illustrated story of a wolf who wanders into the city, looking for new friends only to find that his appearance frightens everyone away. It would be interesting to explore this alongside Emily Gravett's Wolves

C. GOURLAY *Tall Story* (2011) David Fickling Books.

This was recommended to me as a book that deals with what it is like to be different and it does so rather cautiously. Bernardo is so tall he is almost a giant. An unusual book full of humour, the clash of cultures and sibling relationships.

Emily GRAVETT is a book artist whose reputation grows in leaps and bounds. Published by Macmillan Childrens Books. Many have received awards. They are very witty and entertaining postmodern picture storybooks.

*The Odd Egg* (2009)

is the age-old story of what emerges from the egg, illustrated charmingly and playing with print and layout.

*Wolves* (2006)

is many things. It makes apparent all the way through that it is a book. It tells the reader many facts about wolves, but the mood changes and the book becomes frightening but the surprise ending pleases children. Has to be experienced to be appreciated.

Sally GRINDLEY and Peter UTTON (illustrator) *Shhh!* (1999) Hodder Children's Books.

I have enjoyed reading this to and with children for many years – all have found it frightening but also reassuring. I love how it specifically and explicitly invites children to remember that they are 'within' the book but can get out. A postmodern picturebook.

Eric HILL *Where's Spot?* (1983) Puffin.

The date shows that this is a children's classic, one of the first lift-the-flap books. A puppy hides in many places and the young reader must lift the flap to see if he is there or not. A game within a book. Hill made many more books in the same vein but this is the best.

M. HOFFMAN and C. BINCH (illustrator) *Amazing Grace* (2007) Frances Lincoln Books.

Grace is a little girl who believes she can do and be anyone. But when she wants to play Peter Pan in the school play, she is not chosen because she is a girl and black. At first she gets downhearted but her strong grandmother presents a solution.

Pat HUTCHINS is one of the foremost authors for young children. Many of her books are published by Red Fox in various sizes and format. See also the section on wordless picturebooks. All her books have delights to offer.

*Don't Forget the Bacon* (2002)

a little boy is sent shopping with a list in his head, but as he is distracted by what he sees he forgets the list. Children find much to identify with.

*Titch* (1997)

the youngest and smallest child in the family resents the fact that he always gets the cast offs. Much for children to relate to here, too.

Shirley HUGHES *Dogger* (2009) Red Fox.

This is a moving everyday story of a child who loses his favourite toy and finds it again. It has delicate illustrations and is much loved by children and remembered by their parents and grandparents!

Mike INKPEN makes mostly humorous books for children which are worth seeking out, such as *The Great Pet Sale* (2006), *The Blue Balloon* (2006) and *Penguin Small* (2006) all published by Hodder Children's Books.

Oliver JEFFERS *The Heart in the Bottle* (2010) HarperCollins Children's Books.

This book explores grief and sorrow sensitively and with great delicacy. The story is of a little girl whose life was full of wonder and then something happened that made her take out her heart and put it in a safe place. The pictures are minimalist.The author/artist has been described as one of the most important and talented writers of children's books and has received many awards. His other books are imbued with the same sensibility.

Judith KERR *The Tiger Who Came to Tea* (2006) HarperCollins Children's Books.

This classic tale is about everyday life into which strolls a tiger who proceeds to eat and drank everything in the house. Gently humourous, it is much loved by children. Kerr is the author of many picturebooks and story books.

Spike and Tonya Lewis LEE and Kadir NELSON (illustrator) *please, baby, please.* (2006) Aladdin Paperbacks.

This delightful picturebook shows the antics of the baby, who rules the roost and drives her mother crazy, but the love between mother and child shines through. Joyous illustrations of this small black girl and her family.

Francesca MARTIN *The Honey Hunters: a traditional African tale* (1994) Walker Books.

A cumulative story of animals wanting to acquire honey and fighting with one another over it. Detailed and visually pleasing illustrations.

David MCKEE *Not Now, Bernard* (1984) Red Fox and *Elmer* (2007) Anderson.

McKee's books deal with real and serious issues in the lives of children: Bernard is ignored by his parents and Elmer is teased for being different. McKee's characters are sometimes human and sometimes animal, but all allow children to identify with them.

Paula METCALF *Mabel's Magical Garden* (2006) Macmillan Children's Books.

With its splendid illustrations this book gently cautions the reader about building imaginary walls around herself.

David MILLS and Derek BRAZELL (illustrator) *Lima's Read Hot Chilli* (1999) Mantra Lingua.

The story of Lima who eats a chilli and then samples all the foods she can find to try and soothe the burning in her mouth. Available in several versions of dual texts in English and another language – in English and Arabic or English and Greek or English and IsiZulu, for example. Mantra Lingua specialises in multilingual books and the Talking Pen.

Pat MORA and Paula BARRAGAN (illustrator) *Love to mama: A Tribute to Mothers.* (2004) Lee and Low Books.

A beautiful and sensitive book of poems written by thirteen poets – all a tribute to mothers, grand-mothers and other caregiving women. The authors come from Mexico, Cuba, Puerto Rico, California and Venezuela. Tender, joyous, celebratory and very moving. Really worth looking at, especially if you have Spanish speaking children in your group

Toby MORISON *Little Louis Takes Off* (2007) Simon and Schuster.

This is the quirky tale of a bird that can't fly so has to take an aeroplane. Full of little visual references, jokes, delights and the familiar.

Andy MULLIGAN is sometimes compared to Lemony Snicket.

*Ribblestrop* (2009) Simon and Schuster Children's Books.

The boarding school of the title, where the adventures of a small bunch of children takes place, is similar to Hogwarts. Will appeal to rebellious children.

Robert MUNSCH and Michael MARTCHENKO (illustrator) *The Paper Bag Princess* (2009) Annick Press.

Elizabeth is no ordinary princess. She is not interested in clothes or jewels or her appearance or marrying the prince. This book is fun and funny and challenges the roles of both boys and girls.

Jill MURPHY *Peace At Last* (2007) MacMillan Children's Books.

This is one of my favourite picturebooks. Poor Mr Bear can't get to sleep because of all the household noises. Repetitive and memorable text, wonderful illustrations and another classic. Murphy wrote many excellent books.

Kveta PAKOVSKA is a remarkable illustrator whose versions of fairy tales (often made with another author) are breathtaking. *Cinderella* (2010) Minedition. Google her books on amazon to find others.

Catherine RAYNER *Ernest*. Macmillan Children's Books.

This is the tale of a big moose with a big problem. He is too large to fit inside the book. What should he do? Playing with the layout of the book and using devices like folded pages the book artist has made a book that will delight young children.

Michael ROSEN is a poet and the author of many fine books, published by Walker Books.

*We're Going on a Bear Hunt* (2009) has fine illustrations by Helen OXENBURY

Was originally a song, now made into a joyous book.

*Michael Rosen's Sad Book* (2011)

Was written when Rosen's son Eddie died and it is one of the most serious, sensitive and significant books on the subject of death written for young people.

M. SALISBURY *Play Pen: new children's book illustration* (2007) Laurence King.

This is a book for adults. It is an update of new children's books evaluating the quality of the illustrations and includes books not only in English. It is a wonderful, beautiful book so if someone wants to buy you a present you might ask for this.

Maurice SENDAK is another featured author and has influenced the lives of many young consumers of his books. The best known of these is *Where the Wild Things Are* which is now 36 years old and was the first book of a trilogy. My children and their children were reared on this book. His books are currently published by Red Fox.

*Where the Wild Things Are* (2000)

The story of Max who is sent to bed without his supper and experiences a series of strange and intoxicating events as he sails away to where the wild things are. Full of extraordinary images, poetic language, and the miraculous comfort of the happy ending, it deals with power and powerlessness, rage and fear and exultation. It was made into an opera by Oliver Knussen and into a film directed by Spike Jonze. Puppets and other small world objects of the characters are also available.

### Outside Over There (2002)

deals with complex emotional feelings young children might experience because of a sense of loss, being replaced, taken for granted, or not appreciated. The illustrations are surreal and disturbing with much that is strange to examine and ponder. It has a happy ending so children can explore their deep and dark feelings through the safety of the narrative and its conclusion.

### Elfrida VIPONT *The Elephant and the Bad Baby* (2011) Puffin.

This newly reprinted joyous moral tale has a repetitive text, detailed illustrations and the memorable journey of a baby who doesn't know how to say thank you. It is a delightful classic and of great appeal to children who may be tempted to be just like that bad baby.

Martin WADDELL is a distinguished author who works with different illustrators to produce books that are witty, often poignant and have great appeal for young children. They are published by Walker Books.

### *The Park in the Dark* (2002) with illustrations by Barbara FIRTH.

Three toys are in the park when it gets dark. Not a wordless book but many narrative possibilities arise from the pictures and the use of space on the page. Issues touched on include fear of the dark.

### *Can't you sleep, little bear?* (2005) with illustrations by BARBARA FIRTH.

Little bear just can't get to sleep, whatever big bear does to try and settle him. This book, too, deals with children's fear of the dark and the illustrations graphically show the powerful and moving bond between the adult and baby.

### Owl Babies (1994) illustrated by Patrick BENSON.

Three owls wait for their mother who has gone to find food. They fear she won't return. But, of course, she does – and brings food. This story, set again in the dark, is about fear of being abandoned. The happy reassuring ending indicates that this fear is so often groundless.

### *Farmer Duck* (1995) with wonderful illustrations by Helen OXENBURY.

Farm animals discover the power they have when they unite against the exploitative farmer.

Vivian WALSH and Otto SEIBOLD (illustrator) are a husband and wife team who have produced some books which are published by Harcourt Children's Books. They include *Gluey: a snail tale* (2002) and *Olive the Reindeer* (1997). The illustrations in these books are eye-catching – as where, in *Gluey*, the artist uses a range of devices such as laminate printing to create a trail of slime.

### Melanie WATT *Chester* (2008) Harper Collins Children's Books.

Chester the cat uses his red pen to make himself the centre of attention on every page of the book. Described as a postmodern picturebook, some find it very entertaining.

### Rosemary WELLS *Noisy Nora* (2000) Puffin.

This book, dealing, like *Not Now, Bernard*, with feelings of jealousy and resentment about being ignored, has an easy to remember rhyming text and a happy ending. In my eyes this is a classic and I am delighted that it has been re-issued.

### Jonah WINTER and Ana JUAN (illustrator) *Frida* (2007) Frances Lincoln.

A picturebook about the artist Frida Kahlo. The quality of the illustrations leaves much to be desired and there is little sense of this amazing woman and her work. Included in this list because some teachers recommend it.

Charlotte ZOLOTOW and William PENE DU BOIS (illustrator) *William's Doll* (1972) Picture Lions.

The title gives it all away, William wants a doll so is teased. Challenges stereotypes about what is appropriate for boys.

## Chapter books or longer books for young children and their older peers and siblings

Please note that some of the books described in the previous section are both chapter books and picturebooks so do refer to both sections.

Jeff BROWN and Tomi UNGERER (illustrator) *Flat Stanley* (2003) Mammoth.

The unlikely and humorous adventures of Stanley Lambchop who wakes up one morning to find himself flattened by a notice board that fell on him in the night. But he finds he can fly like a kite and slip through the gaps in a grid in the road. An ideal starter story for a child wanting something slightly more complex and longer than a traditional picturebook.

Frances Hodgson BURNETT *The Secret Garden* (2020) Templar.

Often described as a children's classic, this was initially published in serial form. Plain and petulant Mary is orphaned by an outbreak of cholera in India, where she had led a sheltered and pampered life. She is sent to be cared for by an elderly widower living in Yorkshire. There the lonely child encounters her sick cousin Colin, is befriended by the chambermaid and her brother and is led into a secret garden by following a robin. It is a story of loneliness, loss, friendship and change. Also available as an audiobook or as a film on DVD.

Lewis CARROLL *Alice's Adventures in WONDERLAND* (2011) Penguin Classic.

The first edition was illustrated by John TENNIEL and published by Macmillan. Walker Illustrated Classics published a well loved-edition with illustrations by Helen OXENBURY. My favourite is the 1988 hardback illustrated by ANTHONY BROWNE, published by Knopf Books for Young Readers. It tells the many stories – magical, funny, serious and sublime – of a little girl who falls through a rabbit hole where she encounters wild and wonderful creatures such as the White Rabbit, the Queen of Hearts, the Mock Turtle and the Mad Hatter. It is full of wit and playful language and is neither moralising nor didactic. For many children it is an introduction to finding adult playfulness in language. My favourite of many film versions is directed by Jonathan Miller for the BBC.

Sharon CREECH *Granny Torrelli Makes Soup* (2004) Bloomsbury.

Set in the kitchen of an American Italian grandmother this is a story about food and relationships. Her books are much liked by children.

Roald DAHL wrote dozens of popular children's books. He is regarded by many as cruel and by others as brilliant. His writing is humorous and gripping and he does know how to catch and hold the attention of young readers. His books are too numerous to list. Many are published by Puffin and many have been made into films, TV series, appear as e-books, audiobooks and CDs.

Cornelia FUNKE *The Thief Lord* (2000) and *The Inkheart Trilogy* (2011) both published by Chicken House.

Her books have been well reviewed and generally well received. She revels in stories which seem to not end and her love of literature comes through the references she makes to what she has read and heard. Themes include magic and danger.

Neil GAIMAN and Dave MCKEAN (illustrator) *The Graveyard Book* (2009) Blooms-bury Publishing.

This creepy story is full of mystery and suspense, humour and terrifying pictures. It starts with a multiple murder and the episodic style allows for being read aloud over a period of time. Has been well reviewed and has great appeal for some children.

Eva IBBOTSON was born in Vienna and had to flee the Nazis. Her sense of pursuit and danger, adventure and freedom run through her books and is probably best known for *The Secret of Platform 13* (2009) and *Journey to the River Sea* (2011) MacMillan Children's Books.

Judith KERR *When Hitler Stole Pink Rabbit* (2008) HarperCollins.

Anna is not sure who Hitler is as the book opens, but through this story, based on the real-life experiences of the author, she finds out soon enough.

Ian LENDLER and Whitney MARTIN (illustrator) *An Undone Fairy Tale* (2005) Simon and Schuster Books for Young Readers

A postmodern picturebook inviting the reader to question aspects of reality – in this case the conventions regarding love, courtship, marriage and gender.

C.S. LEWIS *The Lion, The Witch and the Wardrobe* (2001) HarperCollins Children's Books. Part of *The chronicles of Narnia*.

A children's classic adventure story which is said to be a metaphor for Christianity.

Michael MORPURGO is the author of many books and passionate defender of narrative, poetry, literature, theatre and the rights of children.

*The Kites Are Flying* (2010) Walker Books.

This is a book which examines serious issues and is aimed at older children although it may be of interest to younger children who are immigrants or refugees or without their parents.

War Horse (2006) Egmont.

The story of what happens to a horse during the First World War. It has been made into a fantastic play featuring remarkable puppets, and also an Oscar nominated film.

Beverley NAIDOO *Journey to Jo'Burg* (2008) HarperCollins Children's Books.

Two children run away from their grandmother in the country to try and find their mother who works as a maid in the city of Johannesburg during the apartheid era. Their baby sister is ill and they fear she will die. In reality she is suffering from starvation. This is the story of their journey from rural poverty to the contrasts of where their mother works and the township in Johannesburg. Naidoo describes the indignities caused by apartheid in an accessible voice. I read the book – a chapter a week – to Year 2 children in London many years ago.

Linda NEWBURY and Pat SMY (illustrator) *Lob* (2011) David Fickling Books.

This short novel, with delicate and rather old fashioned illustrations, draws children into the world of nature and touches on loss, hope and the past. Poetic and sensitive, it is admired by critics and children.

Katherine PATERSON *Bridge to Terabithia* (2007) HarperCollins.

Jesse has few friends at school, loves to draw and dreams of being the fastest kid in the class. He is the only boy in his poor five-child family. His life changes when Leslie moves in next door – her family have money, a television and just one child. Together the children create an imaginary land called Terabithia.

Philip PULLMAN is possibly best known for *His dark materials* trilogy (2008). The books that make up the trilogy are *Northern Lights, Subtle Knife* and *Amber Spyglass* Scholastic.

The poetic, mesmerising and intricately plotted tales deal with complex and serious issues where the real and the fantastic merge and part. Written for older children but certainly accessible to some younger children.

Louis SACHER *Louis Holes* (2000) Bloomsbury Publishing.

Sacher is an American author with a gift for understanding the minds of children and they find his books entertaining and relevant. The books are witty and compelling.

Jon SCIESZKA and Lane SMITH (illustrator) *The True Story of the 3 Little Pigs* (1991) Picture Puffin.

This book allows the reader to take the part of the wolf rather than the pigs and begin to ask questions about fairness and justice. It turns the expected upside down and inside out.

Andy STANTON *You're a Bad Man, Mr Gum* (2006) Egmont Books.

The first of the books about a truly nasty old man and his adventures and the people he encounters. There are evil characters, heroes, a dog, smells, food and lots more. Stanton was a stand-up comic before becoming a writer and his chapter books with pictures are full of jokes. They have received many awards and offer children much to relate to.

Eugene TRIVIZAS and Helen OXENBURY *The Three Little Wolves and the Big Bad Pig* (1997) Margaret K.McElderry Books.

The familiar tale is turned inside out with the wolves being small and defenceless and the pig big and bad. The author, like Scieska, invites the reader to take on different perspectives about events.

Jacqueline WILSON And Nick SHARRATT (illustrator) *Tracey Beaker* (2011) Yearling.

Possibly her best known book. Said to be the most successful writer for children, Wilson addresses issues such as being orphaned, fostered, rejected, sent away, feeling unloved, lonely, frightened, abused and special. Some characters are active participants in the tragedies affecting them and find ways of dealing with them through dreaming, imagination and acting out.

Benjamin ZEPHANIA *Refugee Boy* (2001) Bloomsbury Publishing.

This is a sophisticated book but some children might benefit from listening to or reading this book because of their own experience. This poet and author is concerned with the real life experiences of black people such as Stephen Lawrence.

## Books in Translation

Note: These are not recommendations, simply the publication details of books mentioned, together with some useful website.

Jeannie BAKER *Mirror* (2010) Walker Books.

John BURNINGHAM and Irina KORSCHUNOW (translator) *Mein Opa und Ich* (1984) Parabel.

John BURNINGHAM, translated by Rolf INHAUSER: authorised by John Burningham *Grosspapa*.(1988) Sauerlander.

Michael GAY *Night Ride* adapted from the French by Margo LUNDELL (1987) L'Ecole des Loisirs.

David MILLS and Derek BRAZELL (illustrator) *Lima's Read Hot Chilli* (1999) Mantra Lingua

## Websites

http://www.uel.ac.uk/education/research/duallanguagebooks/

http://www.hvec.org.uk/

http://www.espresso.co.uk/services/primary/index.html

http://www.primarylanguage.org.uk/primary_languages.aspx

http://www.bbc.co.uk/cbeebies/drilldown/stories/2/6/1/

## Controversy in and about books

Note: Books in which controversy is encountered appear in previous sections.

Anthony BROWNE *Voices in the Park* (1999) Transworld Publishers.

Four people in a park and we see the park and what happens there through the eyes of four people: bossy woman, a sad man, a lonely boy and a young girl. Multilayered and offering endless opportunities for talk and reflection and a rare book about adult snobbery for young children.

Linda DE HAAN and Stern NIJLAND, *King & King* (2002) Tricycle Press.

A prince falls in love with another prince, rather than the expected princess.

Tomie DE PAOLA *Oliver Button is a Sissy* (1990) Sandpiper.

Oliver loves to read and paint and tap-dance – things which are not considered to be suitable for boys so is teased and othered. A book dealing with gender stereotyping and with being teased.

Marcus EWART and Rex RAY (illustrator) *10,000 Dresses* (2008) Seven Stories Press.

Bailey loves dresses – all kinds of dresses – and dreams about them, but no one wants to hear about his dreams because he is a boy. Then he meets an older girl and the two begin to make dresses together. A modern fairy tale with a happy ending.

Carolivia HERRON and Joe CEPEDA (illustrator) *Nappy Hair* (1999) Dragonfly Books.

This controversial book, using call and response in celebrating Brenda's wonderfully wild hair, created havoc in middle America, being rejected by black families who felt that aspects of being black were being mocked rather than celebrated as the author and illustrator intended. Have a look for yourselves.

Emily GRAVETT *Wolves* (2006) Macmillan Children's Book.

A witty, entertaining postmodern picturebook.

Cheryl KILODAVIS and Suzanne DE SIMONE (illustrator) *My Princess Boy* (2011) Simon and Schuster.

Dyson loves sparkly pink things. He usually wears jeans and sometimes like to wear a tiara, like a princess, even when he is climbing trees. A book about bullying and discrimination.

Ian LENDLER and Whitney MARTIN (illustrator) *An Undone Fairy Tale* (2005) Simon and Schuster Books for Young Readers

A postmodern picturebook using different features to invite children to arrive at their own conclusions.

Lenore LOOK and Stephen JOHNSON (illustrator) *Love as Strong as Ginger* (1999) Atheneum.

A truly beautiful and thought-provoking book dealing with the world of work for the poor with unusual honesty about the conditions. The relationship between the child and her grandmother is portrayed with sensitivity and the love between them is apparent. Beautiful pastel illustrations. A treat!

Bernard MOST *The Cow that Went Oink* (2003) Harcourt Brace.

A cow that can only say oink is laughed at by the other cows. She meets a pig who can only say moo and they become friends and teach each other their 'languages' A soft way of dealing with bilingualism but humorous and liked by children.

Leslea NEWMAN and Carol THOMPSON (illustrator) *Daddy, Papa and Me* (2009) Tricycle Books.

Written for very young children in rhythmic text this books shows a small child spending the day with parents, both daddies.

Leslea NEWMAN and Carol THOMPSON (illustrator) *Mommy, Mama and Me* (2009) Tricycle Books.

You will guess what this is about.

Leslea NEWMAN and Diana SOUZA (illustrator) *Heather has Two Mommies* (2000) Alyson Books.

Said to be the first book for children written about a same sex family setting, it is the story of a little girl who discovers all the different kinds of families her friends come from and explores the rich diversity of family structures.

Gary PAULSEN *The Tortilla Factory* (1998) Voyager Books.

Beautifully illustrated but romanticised and idealised representation of the work of immigrant factory workers.

Jon SCIESZKA and Lane SMITH (illustrator) *The True Story of the 3 Little Pigs* (1991) Picture Puffin.

Eugene TRIVIZAS and Helen OXENBURY *The Three Little Wolves and the Big Bad Pig* (1997) Margaret K.McElderry Books.

## Other literature and narrative resources
### websites
www.clpe.co.uk

The Centre for Literacy in Primary Education, Webber Street, SE1 8QW is a good place for information about books. They run many excellent courses, have a library and a research base and staff who are informed and helpful.

www.guardian.co.uk/childrens-books-site

The *Guardian's* children's book site is designed specifically for children to take control of exploring books and stories. Easy to access and popular with children. A worthwhile resource for children, with age-related sections, reviews, news and competitions.

## Children's bookshops

The Golden Treasury (www.thegoldentreasury.co.uk/)
29 Replingham Road, Southfields, London SW18 5LT

Children's Bookshop
29 Fortis Green Road
Muswell Hill, London N10 3HP

Victoria Park Books (www.victoriaparkbooks.co.uk)
174 Victoria Park Road, Hackney, London E8 7HD

Tales on Moon Lane (www.talesonmoonlane.co.uk/
25 Half Moon Lane, Herne Hill
London SE24 9JU

Willesden Bookshop (www.willesdenbookshop.co.uk/)
– specialising in multicultural children's books.

Willesden Green Library Centre,
95 High Road
London NW10 4QU

The Lion and Unicorn Bookshop (www.lionunicornbooks.co.uk/)
19 King Street, Richmond, TW9 1ND

Fidra books (www.fidrabooks.com/)
219 Bruntsfield Place, Edinburgh EH10 4DH

Search online to find whether there is a specialist children's bookshop in your area.

## Children's Theatre

### London

The Little Angel Theatre
The Polka Children's Theatre
The Puppet Theatre Barge
The Tricycle Theatre
The Unicorn Theatre

### Manchester

The Royal Exchange Theatre

### Glasgow

Pzazz Children's Theatre

### Birmingham

Birmingham Children's Theatre

# Bibliography

Note: In this bibliography you will sometimes find what look like incomplete entries for example, some without dates of publication. These refer primarily to people writing about aspects of the oral tradition who publish online or in journals which are not necessarily regarded as academic so don't conform to the features of referencing.

Ahlberg, A cited in Moss, G (1990) Metafiction and the poetics of children's literature. in *Children's Literature Association Quarterly* 15 (2)

Ahmed Ali Jimale The Somali Oral Tradition and the Role of Storytelling in Somalia. in *Somaliland Cyberspace*. (http://www.mbali.info/doc255.htm) accessed 11/02/11

Alarcon in Mora, P (ed) (2001) *Love to Mama: a tribute to mothers*. New York: Lee and Low Books

Arizpe, E and Styles, M (2003) *Children reading pictures: interpreting visual texts*. London and New York: Routledge.

Arthur, L (2001) Popular Culture and Early Literacy Learning. *Contemporary Issues in Early Childhood* 2(3) p 295-308

Ashliman, D.L. website Pitt Source: Karl Gander, 'Der fortgelaufene Eierkuchen,' Niederlausitzer Volkssagen, vornehmlich aus dem Stadt- und Landkreise Guben (Berlin: Deutsche Schriftsteller-Genossenschaft, 1894), no. 319, p 122-123.

Bader, M (1976) *American Picture Books: From Noah's Ark to the Beast Within*. New York: Macmillan.

Bakhtin, M (1981) *The Dialogic Imagination: Four Essays* in Holquist (ed) (translated Emerson and Holquist). Austin and London: University of Texas Press. (written during 1930s)

Bakhtin, M (1990) *Art and answerability: Early Philosophical Essays*. Austin, Texas: University of Texas Press

Baring-Gould(1886) Appendix to William Henderson, *Notes on the Folk Lore of the Northern Counties of England*. London: Longmans, Green, and Company

Bearne, E. and V. Watson (eds) (1994) *Where Texts and Children Meet*. London and New York: Routledge.

Bettelheim, B (1976/1995 reprint) *The Uses of Enchantment: The Meaning and Importance of Fairy Tales*. London: Penguin Psychology.

Blaise, M (2005) *Playing it Straight: Uncovering Gender Discourses in the Early Childhood Classroom*. London and New York: Routledge.

Bourdieu, P (1977) *Outline of a theory in Practice*. Cambridge: Cambridge University Press.

Brostrom, S (2002) Children Tell Stories. *European Early Childhood Education Research Journal* 10 (1) p85-97

Browne, A (1994) Making Picture Books in M. Styles, E. Bearne and V. Watson (eds) (1994) *The Prose and the Passion: Children and their reading*. London and New York: Cassell

Browne, N (1999) *Young Children's Literacy Development and the Role of Televisual Texts*. London: Falmer Press

Bruner, J (1990) *Acts of Meaning*. Cambridge, Mass and London: Harvard University Press.

Bruner, J (2002) *Making Stories: Law, Literature, Life*. Cambridge, Mass and London: Harvard University Press

Bruner, J and Lucariello, J (1989) 'Monologue as Narrative Recreation of the World' in Nelson, K (ed) *Narratives from the Crib*. Cambridge. Mass: Harvard University Press

Carr, N (2011) The Dreams of Readers in *Stop What You're Doing and Read This!* Mark Haddon, Michael Rosen, Zadie Smith, Carmen Callil, Jeanette Winterson, Tim Parks, Blake Morrison, Mary-anne Wolf, Nicholas Carr and Jane Davis (authors) London: Vintage Books

Chambers, A. *Tell me (Children Reading and Talk)* (1993) with *The Reading Environment* (1991) jointly published 2011. Stroud: Thimble Press.

Chapra, M in Mora, P (ed) (2001) *Love to Mama: a tribute to mothers*. New York: Lee and Low Books

Ching, S (2005) Multicultural Children's Literature as an Instrument of Power. *Language Arts* 83(2) p128-136

Chomsky, N (1968) *Language and Mind*. New York: Harcourt Brace and World

Chukovsky, K (1963) *From Two to Five*. Berkeley, Los Angeles, London: University of Cambridge Press

Coates, E. (2002) 'I forgot the sky!' Children's Stories Contained within Their Drawings. *International Journal of Early Years Education* 10 (1) p21-35

Cooper, PM (2005) Literacy learning and pedagogical purpose in Vivian Paley's 'storytelling curriculum'. *Journal of Early Childhood Literacy* 5(3) p229-251

Crawford, PA and Hade, DD (2000) Inside the picture, outside the frame: Semiotics and the reading of wordless picture books. *Journal of Research in Childhood Education* 15 (1) p66-80

Davies, MD and R. Oittinen (eds) (2008) *Whose Story? Translating the Verbal and the Visual in literature for young readers*. Cambridge Scholars Publishing.

Dayrell, E (1910) at http://www.sacred-texts.com/afr/fssn/fsn20.htm

deMarrais, K.B, Nelson, P.A. and Baker, J.H. (1994) Meaning in Mud: Yup'ik Eskimo Girls at Play in J.L Roopnarine, J.E.Johnson, and F.H. Hooper (eds) *Children's play in diverse cultures*. Albany: State University of New York Press.

Donoghue, E (2010) *Room*. Picador

Dunn, J (1988) *The Beginnings of Social Understanding*. Cambridge, Mass: Harvard University Press

Dyson, AH (1997) *Writing Superheroes: Contemporary Childhood, Popular Culture and Classroom Literacy*. New York and London: Teachers College Press.

Eagleton, T (1983) *Literary Theory: an Introduction*. Minnesota: University of Minnesota Press.

Eagleton, T (2000) *The Idea of Culture*. London: Wiley-Blackwell; First Edition edition

Elkin, J (1976) *Books for the Multi-Racial Classroom: A Select List of Children's Books, Showing the Backgrounds of India, Pakistan and the West Indies*. Pamphlet No 17. Second Edition. London: Youth Librarians Group.

Foucault, M (1994) *The Order of Things: An Archaeology of the Human Sciences*. London: Vintage Books

Fox, C (1993) *At the Very Edge of the Forest: the influence of literature on storytelling by children*. London and New York: Cassell

Fox, G (1996) Reading Picture Books ..How To? in M.Styles, E. Bearne and V. Watson (eds)(1996) *Voices Off: Texts, contexts and readers.* London and New York: Cassell

Garvey, C (1977) *Play.* Cambridge, Mass: Harvard University Press.

Geyh P (2003) Assembling Postmodernism: Experience, Meaning and the Space in-Between. *College Literature* 30(2) p1-29

Giroux, H. A. Animating Youth: the Disnification of Children's Culture. *European Medi@Culture-Online.* http://www.european-mediaculture.org.

Giugni, M (2006) Conceptualising Goodies and Baddies through Narratives of Jesus and Super-man. *Contemporary Issues in Early Childhood* 7(2) p 97-108

Gonzalez in Mora, P (ed) (2001) *Love to Mama: a tribute to mothers.* New York: Lee and Low Book

Gregory, E and Biarnes, J. (1994) Tony and Jean-Francois: Looking for sense in the strangeness of school in H. Dombey, H and M.M. Spencer (eds) *First Steps Together.* Stoke-on-Trent: Trentham

Gregory, E, Long, S and Volk, D (2004) Syncretic literacy studies: starting points. in E. Gregory, S. Long, S and D. Volk (eds) *Many Pathways to Literacy.* New York and London: RoutledgeFalmer

Halmari, H and Smith, W (1994) Code switching and register shift: Evidence from Finnish-English child bilingual conversion. *Journal of Pragmatics* 21: p427-45

Howe, M.J. Bronte Juvenilia www.fathom.com/feature/122071 accessed 11/04/2011

Kelly, C (2004) Buzz Lightyear in the nursery. In E.Gregory. S.Long and D.Volk(eds) *Many Pathways to Literacy: young children learning with siblings, grandparents, peers and communities.* New York and London: Routledge

Kenner, C (2003) *Bilingual children's uses of popular culture in text-making.* ESRC Research Seminar Series, Children's Literature and Popular Culture Conference, University of Sheffield 2003-4

Kenner C and Kress G (2003) The multisemiotic resources of biliterate children. *Journal of Early Childhood Literacy* 3(2) p179-202.

Kenner, C. (2004) Living in simultaneous worlds: difference and integration in bilingual script-learning. *International Journal of Bilingual Education and Bilingualism.*

Klein, G (1993) *Education towards Race Equality.* New York and London: Cassell

Kress, G (1997) *Before Writing: Rethinking the paths to literacy.* London and New York: Routledge

Kusugak, M (2006) *The Curse of the Shaman: A Marble Island Story.* Harper Collins cited in Schwarz, J. Transmitting Oral Culture to the Page: the Emergence of Inuit Children's Books. http://www.ibbycompostela2010.org/descarregas/10/10_IBBY2010_7.pd

Kwan-terry, A (1992) Code-switching and code-mixing: The case of a child learning English and Chinese simultaneously. *Journal of Multilingual and Multicultural Development* 13 p243-59

Lehr, S (ed) (1995) *Battling Dragons: Issues and controversy in children's literature.* Portsmouth: Heinemann.

Look (1999) see Building Your Collection

Lucca, C in Mora, P (ed) (2001) *Love to Mama: a tribute to mothers.* New York: Lee and Low Books

Marsh, J and Millard, E (2000) *Literacy and Popular Culture: Using children's culture in the class-room.* London, Thousand Oaks, CA and New Delhi: Paul Chapman Publishing.

Marsh, J (2004) The Techno-Literacy Practices of Young Children. *Journal of Early Childhood Research* 2(1) p51-66

Marsh, J, Brooks, G, Hughes, J, Ritchie. L, Roberts, S and Wright K (2005) *Digital beginnings: Young children's use of popular culture, media and the new technologies.* www.esmeefairbairn.org.uk/docs/DigitalBeginiinsReport.pdf accessed throughout early 2011

Marsh, J. and Willett, R (2010) Mega mash-ups and remixes in the cultural borderlands: Emergent findings from the ethnographic studies of playground games and rhymes in two primary schools. Presented at Children's Playground Games in the Age of New Media Interim Conference Feb 2010, London Knowledge Lab.

Marsh, J (in preparation) Children as knowledge brokers. To be submitted to *Children and Society*.

Marsh, J and Bishop JC (in preparation ) 'We're playing 'Jeremy Kyle!': Television talk shows in the playground.' To be submitted to *International Journal of Learning and Media*.

Martin, W and Dombey, H. (2002) Finding a Voice: Language and Play in the Home Corner. *Language and Education* 16(1) p48-61

Meek, M (1991) *On Being Literate*. London: The Bodley Head

Meek, M How Texts Teach What Readers Learn (1988) Stroud: Thimble Press.

Meek, M (2001) The Englishness of English Children's Books in Meek, M (ed) *Children's Literature and National Identity*. Stoke on Trent, Trentham

Mendoza, J and Reese, D. Examining Multicultural Picture Books for the Early Childhood Programme: Possibilities and Pitfalls. *Early Childhood Research and Practice* 3(2) (http://ecrp.uiuc.ed/v3n2/mendoza.html) accessed 13/02/11

Millard, E (2004) *Transformative Practitioners, Transformative Practice: Teacher Working with Popular Culture in the Classroom*. ESRC Research Seminar Series, Children's Literature and Popular Culture, University of Sheffield, 2002-2004

Miller, P (1995) Narrative practices: their role in socialization and self-construction in U. Neisser and R. Fivush (eds) *The Remembering Self: Construction and Accuracy in the Self Narrative*. Cambridge: Cambridge University Press.

Minns, H (1990) *Read it to me now! Learning at home and at school*. London: Virago

Mora, P (ed) (2001) *Love to Mama: a tribute to mothers*. New York: Lee and Low Books

Moss, G (1990) Metafiction and the Poetics of Children's Literature. *Children's Literature Association Quarterly* 15(2) p50-52

Mutchler in Mora, P (ed) (2001) *Love to Mama: a tribute to mothers*. New York: Lee and Low Books

Naidoo, B (1995) Undesirable Publications: *A Journey to Jo'burg* in Lehr, S (ed) *Battling Dragons: Issues and Controversy in Children's Literature*. Portsmouth: Heinemann

Nathenson-Mejia, S and Excamila, K (2003) Connecting With Latino Children: Bridging Cultural Gaps with Children's Literature. *Bilingual Research Journal* 27(1) p101-113

Nikolajeva, M and Scott, C (2006) *How Picturebooks Work*. New York, London: Routledge.

Nodelman, P (1992) Literary theory and children's literature. The Other: Orientalism, Colonialism and Children's Literature. *Children's Literature Association Quarterly* 17 (1) p29-33

Nodelman, P (2008) *The Hidden Adult: Defining Children's Literature*. Baltimore: The Johns Hopkins University Press.

Ochs, E (1996) Linguistic resource for socializing humanity in H. Gumperz and S. Levinson (eds) *Rethinking Linguistic relativity*. New York: Cambridge University Press

Opie, I and Opie (1959 Reprint Marina Warner 2001) *The Lore and Language of Schoolchildren*. New York: New York Review of Books.

Ong, JW (1982) *Orality and Literacy: The Technologizing of the Word*. London: Methuen

O'Neil, K (2010) Once Upon Today: Teaching for Social Justice with Postmodern Picturebooks. *Children's Literature in Education* 41: p 40-51

O'Sullivan E (1998) Losses and gains in the translation of children's literature: Some remarks on the translation of humour in the books of Aidan Chambers (Aidan Bell, trans). in E.D.Keyser (ed) *Children's Literature* 26 p185-200

O'Sullivan, E(2006) Translating Pictures in Lathey, G (ed) *The Translation of Children's Literature: a Reader.* Clevedon, New York and Ontario: Multilingual Matters

Paley, V.G. (1981) *Wally's Stories: Conversations in the Kindergarten.* Cambridge, Mass and London: Harvard University Press

Paley, V.G. (1988) *Bad Guys Don't Have Birthdays: Fantasy Play at Four.* Chicago and London: University of Chicago Press

Paley, V.G. (1999) *The Kindness of Children.* Cambridge, Mass and London: Harvard University Press

Pantaleo S (2010) Mutinous Fictions: Narrative and Illustrative Metalepsis in Three Postmodern Picturebooks. *Children's Literature in Education* 41 p12-27

Paugh, A.L. (2005) Multilingual play: Children's code-switching, role play and agency in Dominica, West Indies. *Language in Society* 34 p63-86

Perrault, C (retold by Angela Carter and illustrated by Jack Zipes) (2008) *The Fairy Tales of Charles Perrault.* London: Penguin Classics

Prout, J. (2005) *The future of childhood.* Abingdon: RoutledgeFalmer

Purushotma, R., Clinton, K., Weigel, M and Robinson. A (2010) *Confronting the Challenges of Participatory Culture: Media Education for the 21st Century* http://newmedialiteracies.org/files/working/NMLWhitePaper.pd accessed 08/03/11

Rosen, H (1984) *Stories and Meanings.* NATE (National Association for the Teaching of English) Papers in Education

Rosen, M (1982) 'Three Papers' in *Becoming our own experts: studies in language and learning made by the talk workshop group at Vauxhall Manor School 1974-79* p378-391

Rosenberg, B (1987) The Complexity of Oral Tradition. *Oral Tradition* 2(1) p73-90

Rowe, A (1996) Voices Off: Wordless Picture Books in M. Styles, E. Bearne and V. Watson (eds) (1996) *Voices Off: Texts, contexts and readers.* London and New York: Cassell

Panteleo, S. 'Reading' Young children's visual Texts. *Early Childhood Research and Practice* 7(1) (http://ecrp.edu/v7n1/pantaleo.html/) accessed 04/02/11

Sachs, H (1972) On the analysability of stories by children in J. Gumperz and D. Hymes (eds) *Directions in Sociolinguistics: the ethnography of communications.* Austin, Texas: Holt, Rinehart and Winston

Said, E (1978) *Orientalism.* London: Vintage Books.

Salisbury, M(2007) *Play Pen: New Children's Book Illustration.* London: Laurence King Publishing

Schwarz, J *Transmitting Oral Culture to the Page: the Emergence of Inuit Children's Books*

Smidt, S (200l) 'All stories that have happy endings have a bad character': a young child responds to televisual texts. *English in Education NATE* 35(2) p25-33

Smidt, S (2004) Sinister storytellers, magic flutes and spinning tops: the links between play and 'popular' culture. *Early Years: An International Journal of Research and Development* 24(1)p75-85

Smidt, S (2006) *The Developing Child in the 21st Century: a global perspective on child development.* London and New York: Routledge

Smidt, S (2009) *Introducing Vygotsky: a guide for practitioners and students in early years education.* London and New York: Routledge

Smidt, S (2011) *Introducing Bruner: a guide for practitioners and students in early years education.* London and New York: Routledge

Smidt, S (2011) *Playing to learn: the role of play in the early years.* London and New York: Routledge.

Sneddon, R (2009) *Bilingual Books Biliterate Children: learning to read through dual language books*. Stoke on Trent and London: Trentham Books in partnership with Mantra Lingua.

Stones, R (2005 new edition) *Don't Pick on Me: How to handle bullying*. London: Piccadilly Press

Styles, M, Bearne, E and Watson, V (eds) (1994) *The Prose and the Passion: Children and their reading*. London and New York: Cassell

Styles, M, Bearne, E and Watson, V (eds) (1996) *Voices Off: Texts, contexts and readers*. London and New York: Cassell

Suarex, V in Mora, P (ed) (2001) *Love to Mama: a tribute to mothers*. New York:Lee and Low Books

Van den Berg, R (undated online publication) *Aboriginal Storytelling and Writing*. (http://docs.google.com/viewer?a=v&q=cache: accessed 11/02/11

Vygotsky, L (1962) *Thought and Language*. Cambridge Mass: MIT Press

Williams, A (2004) 'Right, get your book bags!: siblings playing school in multiethnic London in E. Gregory *et al* (eds) *Many Pathways to Literacy: Young children learning with siblings, grandparents, peers and communities*. New York and London: RoutledgeFalmer.

Wissler, C and Duvall, D.C. *Mythology of the Blackfoot Indians*. New York: Anthropological Papers of the American Museum of Natural History (1908) 2 (1) p19

Wollman-Bonilla, J (1998) Outrageous Viewpoints: Teachers' Criteria for Rejecting Works of Children's Literature. *Language Arts* 75(4) p287-295 NATE

http://www.crickcrackclub.com/CRICRACK/ARTTRADF.HTM (accessed 10/01/11)

http://dictionary.reference.com/browse/literature (accessed 13/01/11).

http://www.pitt.edu/~dash/folktexts.html (accessed 15/02/11)

# Index

abandonment 38, 47
adapting a story 38, 45, 71
adopting roles 139, 143-147
affect 22, 135
Africa 4, 9-11, 32-3, 37, 75, 82, 101, 121, 130, 142
Afrikaans 33
agency 117, 128
Afghanistan 33
Ahlberg, J and A 62, 66, 101, 119, 155-6, 171
*Alice in Wonderland* 323, 164
alliteration 105
alternatives 9, 107, 118
analysis, analysing 8, 23, 30, 34, 74, 79, 84, 86, 90, 109, 119, 120, 121, 126, 129-132, 135, 145
Angria 140-142
*Animal Farm* 8, 68,163
Arabic 54, 95, 104, 105,
artist 16, 21, 24, 43-51, 53, 54, 57, 61, 65, 68, 79, 81, 97, 118, 119
Australia 20, 24, 33, 97,104
author/authors 18, 24, 45, 50, 57, 58, 59, 61, 66, 68, 75, 76, 79, 93, 99, 114, 116, 119, 121, 129, 130, 131, 142, 144, 147, 151, 155-8, 160-172
authority 116, 129, 144, 147

Bakhtin, Michael 47, 97-98, 171
    handed to child 54, 84, 101
Barker, Keith 62, 141

a beginning, beginnings 9, 38, 40, 46, 47, 52, 73, 74, 82, 126, 135-6
beholder 21, 45, 48, 50, 54, 79, 99, 156
Belloc, Hillaire 22, 153
Bettelheim, Bruno 34, 109, 171
bilingual 13, 88, 104, 146, 168
Blackfoot Indians 136, 176
book making 24, 29, 30, 31, 44-48, 49, 55, 67, 72-75, 83, 103, 105, 122, 135, 143
bookshops 49, 52, 67, 70, 80, 155, 169
Bourdieu, P 85-86, 171
boys 70, 83, 85, 88, 90, 92, 113, 137, 150
Bronte children 130, 140-142
Brostrom, Stig 134
Brown, Naima 23
Browne, Anthony 57-58, 63-67, 112, 115, 157, 164, 167, 171, 172
Bruner, Jerome 7-10, 74, 126-129, 132-134, 143-144, 158, 172, 175
**Building Your Collection 153-169**
bullying 92, 167, 176
Buzz Lightyear 12
Burningham, John 59, 60, 65, 99, 100, 158, 166

Canada 33, 158
canonical 8, 128, 133
Carle, Eric 57, 158

celebration of difference 67, 122
challenge/task 37, 40, 53, 72, 73, 75, 79, 116, 125, 134, 150
chants 14, 34, 62
chapter books 71-80
characters 8, 9, 34, 40, 51, 62, 67, 72-75, 77, 83, 85, 135, 140-144, 146, 155, 157, 161, 162, 166
childhood 3-4, 14-16, 84, 89, 100, 116, 141, 155, 171-175
child's work 24-5, 39-40, 53-54, 90-91, 105
Ching, Stuart 121, 172
choices 52, 91, 106, 147
Chomsky, Noam 125-126, 172
Chukovsky, Kornei 59, 139-140, 144, 150, 151, 172
class 38, 85, 113, 115, 146
cognitive achievement, skills 134, 146
collaboration 128, 143
colours, use and significance 20-21, 24, 43, 44, 64, 98, 158
comics 7, 45, 65, 81, 83, 166
communication 11-12, 29, 50, 127
communities 102, 104
    diverse 99-101
    of storymakers 73
community languages *see* home/community languages

comparisons 19, 33, 60, 76, 91

complex books, stories 25, 50, 58, 68, 73, 74, 79, 86, 133

computer games 82, 83, 118

concepts 11, 16, 25, 95

context 4, 17, 22, 31-33, 47, 49, 59-60, 94-5, 98, 105, 126-7, 134, 146

copyright 119

covers 20, 51, 52, 54, 99, 119

Crawford, P and Hade, D 51, 172

creation myths 36, 38

Cric Crac 39, 41, 154

cultural
    aberration 133
    awareness 121
    capital 85-86
    heroes 35
    knowledge/learning 105, 146
    norms 39 stories 8, 11, 101
    tools 10, 11, 19, 50

culture-free 68, 97

culture-specific 52, 82, 126

cumulative stories 36, 59, 157, 161

death 63, 84, 99, 109, 133, 144, 162

decoding 49, 74

de Marrais 39, 172

dialect 7, 121

dialogue, dialogic 8, 23-4, 41, 44, 52,58, 99, 150, 155, 171

diaries 22, 83, 159

difference and othering 116-117
    celebration of/respect for 14, 67, 91, 122

difficult issues/themes 34, 67, 69, 73-74, 105

digital 5, 82, 94, 114, 118, 173

discrimination 6, 85, 167

Disney, Walt 88-89

Dominica 146-147, 175

Donaldson, Julia 46, 58, 159

dual text books 13, 95,103-106,155, 161, 167, 176
    see also Chapter 8 and Building Your Collection

Dunn, Judy 8, 114, 134, 172

DVDs 5, 25, 68, 94, 99, 154. 164

Dyson, A. H 84, 167, 172

Eagleton, Terry 7, 122, 172

education 6, 19, 24, 72, 102, 129, 144, 147

educators 22, 72, 81, 83, 86, 103, 123, 148, 158

an end, endings 9, 30, 38, 40, 46, 47, 52, 73, 74, 103, 135-6, 150, 175

endpapers 49, 98, 119

English
    language 13, 18, 21, 33, 36, 39, 48, 49, 54, 55, 57 70, 85, 88, 90, 92, 94, 95, 100, 103
    non-standard 85
    print 47, 104, 105, 106, 113

episodes 30, 83, 99

equity 38, 85

expectations 67, 126

experts 89, 117, 175

explanation 34, 35, 78, 80, 100, 127, 133

exploitation 57, 68

exploration 10, 34, 51, 86, 139, 140

expression 5, 44, 52, 53, 54, 99, 135, 145

fables see also traditional tales 35, 38, 153, 154

fairness 38, 77, 166

fairy tales 34, 109, 132, 139, 140, 148, 153-155, 162, 171, 175

families 33, 68, 69, 73, 82, 85, 86, 103, 104, 112, 116, 117, 122, 134, 146, 167, 168

fantasy 4, 65, 67, 73, 90, 134, 139, 156
    world 9, 84, 140, 154

fear 8, 9, 34, 48, 53, 60, 62, 63, 69, 72, 74, 79, 105, 123, 134, 146, 147, 150, 156, 162, 163, 165

feelings 4, 8, 12, 16, 19, 20, 30, 34, 39, 43, 50, 60, 68, 69, 72-74, 77, 84, 112, 114, 123, 128, 134, 135, 140, 146, 156, 163

film 5-6, 9-15, 23-24, 43, 45, 48, 50, 52, 64-5, 68, 72, 78-83, 87-92, 94, 96, 99, 109, 118, 162, 164 see also Chapter 2 and Chapter 8

Finnish 77, 146, 173

first language 18, 55, 92, 94, 101, 104, 105, 125, 146, 147

fixed 11,16, 29, 33, 43, 45, 57, 114, 115, 118, 133

folk tales 31, 34-5, 37, 139,140, 153-5

formats 25, 69, 74, 83, 103, Bruner's ideas on 126-127, 158

Foucault, Michael 129

Fox, Carol 12

framing images 44-45, 52

Fyleman, Rose 21-2

games 11, 34, 68, 89-90, 127, 128
    electronic 82, 83, 87, 94, 118

Garvey, C 144, 173

gender 12, 83, 85, 88, 92, 116, 118, 146, 165
    roles/ stereotyping 39, 84, 88, 117, 167

generation 16, 31, 33, 34, 38, 125

genre 22, 23, 34, 43, 68, 96, 112, 146

gesture 12, 52, 133, 145, 146

Geyh, Paula 113

girls 12,35, 39, 70, 83, 85, 90, 92, 113, 137, 141, 145, 162, 172
Giroux, Henry 88-89, 173
grammar 125-127, 130-131
Gravett, Emily 61, 119, 159, 160, 167
Gregory, Eve 101-102, 103, 173, 176
Grindley, Sally 61, 160

habitus 86-87
Hebrew 54, 95
Heide, Florence 44
Hellsing, Lennart 93
hidden narratives 54
high culture 3, 5-7, 14, 81-82 see also Chapter 8
history 5, 10, 31, 45
home/community languages 14, 41, 90, 93, 102-103, 106, 147
Hughes, Martin 114
humour 47, 67, 105, 141, 159-161, 165, 174

icon 98 see also chapter 2
idealisation of childhood, people and settings 4, 31, 113, 155, 168
identity 17, 87, 88, 91,101, 122, 142, 147, 174
illustrations 18, 52, 68, 69, 103, 112, 154-165, 168
illustrators 4, 18, 50, 53, 65, 154-168
images 4,6,12, 14, 16-18, 20-22, 24-25, 34, 43-55, 62, 64, 57-71, 73, 81, 88, 92, 101, 104, 105, 118, 142, 151, 154, 158, 162
imaginary 40, 46, 63, 65, 73, 84, 87, 139, 140, 142, 146, 150, 165
imagination 4, 15, 20, 21, 24, 58, 65, 88, 89, 99, 139, 141, 159, 166
imitation 19, 125, 126
implied reader 18, 46-47, 58, 60, 64-65, 101

in role 34, 38, 83-91, 139-153
indeterminacy 114-115
index 98
interpretation 16, 20, 24, 31, 43-45, 114, 151
intersemiotic translation 98 see also Chapter 2
intertextuality 52, 62,105
intonation 29, 127
Inuit 33, 39, 173, 175

jealousy 74, 109, 163
jingles 10, 29
joining in 13, 32. 38, 60, 61, 65, 69, 112, 117, 127, 156
jokes 47, 66, 105, 161, 166
judgment 71, 72, 88, 91

Kenner, C 87, 90, 101,173
kinship 39, 122
Kress, Gunther 16-22, 91, 101, 173
Kusugak, M 33, 173
Kwan-Terry 146, 173

language acquisition 86, 125-128, 146-147
languages 146, 173 see also first language
Larrick, Nancy 66
Latino children 103, 122
layout 46, 61, 98, 156, 160, 162
Lear, Edward 12, 22, 153
Lee, Suzy 44-46
Lewis, C.S. 76, 165
library 13, 41, 67, 70, 80, 89, 119, 147, 159, 168, 169
lilt 40, 131, 151, 154
linguist 15, 112, 150
listener 8, 12, 21, 23, 31, 38, 40, 58, 78, 80, 118, 132, 136
listening 10, 16, 19, 31, 32, 39, 40, 65, 74, 78, 79, 83, 87, 88, 92, 96, 127, 144, 149, 150, 166
to stories 7, 29, 39, 40, 71, 79, 128, 133
literal 20, 94, 112, 143

literature, definition of 4-7, 11-12, 93
loneliness 34, 68, 74, 85, 112, 142, 164
long ago 40, 103, 117
loss 35, 74, 77, 141, 163, 164, 165
lullabies 40
Lucariello, Joan 9, 132-133

Macaulay, David 11, 111-113
making meaning/meaning-making 30, 39, 41, 57, 72, 75, 88, 94, 97, 101, 105, 126, 139, 43 see also Chapter 2
making own signs and images 17, 20-22, 73, 151
Mantra Lingua 67, 103, 161, 167
Marsh, Jackie 82-83, 89-90
Marx, Karl 85
meaning 50, 53, 62-63, 70, 79, 87, 90, 95, 103, 151
Meek, Margaret 6, 39, 40, 47, 59, 65, 101
members 79, 81, 101, 102, 146
memory/memorising 4, 11, 31, 39, 50, 53, 65,73, 75, 80, 96, 122, 134, 155
messages 34, 50, 74, 103, 132
metafiction 61, 112, 119
metalepsis 118-119
metaphor 15, 20-21, 60, 73, 74, 76-77, 105, 165
migrants 105, 165
Millard, E 83
Miller, Peggy 133
Mills, David 18, 67,161, 167
modelling 85, 126, 127
morality/morals 35, 38, 146
Morpurgo, Michael 72, 78, 123, 144, 165
motives 30, 31, 53, 114
Mozart 7, 82
multilayering 55, 65, 142, 157, 167

multimodal/multimodality 20, 83, 92
multiple perspectives 52, 91,
Murphy, Jill 60, 162
music/musicals 23, 33, 82, 91, 96, 97, 99, 109, 143, 151, 155

Naidoo, Beverley 75, 123, 165
name-calling 117, 128
narrators 23, 45, 47, 48, 69, 84, 101, 128, 130, 132, 137
negotiation 91, 139, 147, 148, 151
Newham Women's Writing Group 103
Nikolajevna and Scott 120
Nodelman, Perry 4, 31, 116
noise 23, 30, 53, 60, 61, 80, 100, 145, 162
nonsense/nonsense rhymes 12, 22, 29, 153, 154
nursery rhymes 6, 34, 62, 105, 153, 154

O'Neil, Kathleen 113-114, 165
O'Sullivan, Emer 99-100
Ochs 147
Ong, Walter 31
online storyteller sites 41
open-ended texts 21, 52, 54, 78
Opie, Iona and Peter 34,155
oral tradition 29-41
orientalism 116
othered/othering 18, 116, 121, 167
The Owl and the Pussy-Cat 22

pace 13, 22, 68, 74, 151
Paley, Vivian Gussin 3, 40, 84, 87, 131, 136, 148-150
Pantaleo, S 120
parallel stories 23, 57, 58, 65, 69, 156, 158
parody 114, 119

Patwa 147-148
Paugh, Amy 146-7
pedagogy 24-25, 40-41, 54-55, 69-70, 72, 80, 90, 106
of narrative 24, 40, 54, 69, 80, 92, 106
of relationships 72
peekaboo games 8, 127, 158
peers 81-83, 105, 122, 135, 147, 148, 164
Peirce, Charles 98
perceptions 20, 104, 151
performance 18, 71, 91, 155
Perrault, Charles 34
perspective of others 52, 85, 91, 114, 129
picturebooks 4, 6, 20-21, 78, 148 see also Chapter 9
in translation 97-99
with words 57-70 see also Chapter 5
wordless 43-55, 143 see also Chapter 4 155-156, 160
pictureless text 71-80 see also Chapter 6
pictures see images
pictures as signs 20, 43-55, 98
play and games 8, 11, 34, 68, 82-83, 87, 89-90, 118, 146 127, 151, 155
role play 83, 87, 127, 139, 142-148, 155 see also Chapter 10
playground culture 11, 34, 39, 155
plot 67, 74, 112, 114, 135, 155, 166
poems 10, 22, 25, 29, 78, 141, 153-154, 161
poetry 5-6, 13, 15, 22, 93, 142, 153, 165
popular culture 3, 5, 7, 14, 81-92
possible worlds 40, 73-74, 94, 112, 139, 146
postmodern picturebooks 109-124, 160, 163, 165, 167 see also Chapter 9

poverty 85, 165
prelinguistic behaviour 127, 128
prediction 11, 34, 73, 75, 128, 144, 159
preferences 22, 25, 87, 91
prejudice 81, 84-85
print 24, 31, 33, 47, 68, 69, 83, 95, 104-106, 160
protonarratives 39, 128
Prout, A 86
psychologist 123, 150
Pullman, Phillip 71, 78, 143, 144, 166
Punjabi 13, 155

Quangle-Wangle's Hat 12

race, racism 84, 85, 89, 146
re-tellings 13, 33, 38, 57, 62, 69, 114, 135
reading direction 24, 45, 47, 95, 98, 104-106,
real and possible/imagined 40, 73-74, 94,112, 139, 143
reflection 73, 86, 129, 142, 159, 167
refugees 78
repetition 23, 31, 33, 51, 58, 59, 60, 66, 73, 112, 127, 156
repetitive text 69, 158, 162, 163
research 8, 51, 82-85, 89, 101, 103, 123, 135-137, 146-147, 167-168
resources 66, 101, 153, 168
response of the adult 17, 48-50, 65, 92
rhyme 3-4, 6-7, 10, 12, 14, 22, 25, 29, 31, 34, 58, 62, 73, 102, 105, 151, 153, 154, 155, 157
rhythm 4, 13, 22, 58, 68, 73, 102, 151, 168
ritual 8, 11, 31, 39, 51, 52, 89, 96, 1-5, 156
Rosen, Harold 29-30

Rosen, Michael 22, 58, 63, 153, 162
Roy Yates Books 103
rule-bound 8, 12, 16, 39
rules of narrative 39, 92, 128, 132-133
Russian 10, 11, 65, 78, 94-5, 97, 118, 150, 154

Sachs, Harvey 30
safe space 147-148
safety of the story/book/narrative 34, 61, 69,
Said, Edward 116
sanitising 99
Saussure 15-16
Schwartz, Joanne 33
screen 23, 48, 64, 82, 87, 90, 94
The Secret Garden 6, 9, 10, 79, 83, 137, 164
Sendak, Maurice 20, 45, 57, 60, 162
sequence 23-24, 30, 36, 43-46, 50, 54, 60, 72, 99, 128, 134, 136,
sexism 84, 85, 89
sexuality 116
Shrek 65
siblings 32, 39, 51, 83, 134, 142, 164
signs 12, 14, 18, 45, 47, 94, 96, 98 see also Chapter 2
simile 60, 73, 76
simultaneous worlds 65
Sneddon, R 102

social capital 86
conditions 98
context 10
conventions 117-118
development 134
institutions 129
networks 68
problems 85
values 85
worlds 95, 128
socialisation 146-147
societies 10, 11, 31, 33, 86
society 6, 31, 80, 81, 82, 85, 86, 95, 139,
Somalia 33
songs 6-7, 10-11, 14, 23, 24, 25, 43, 47, 40, 87, 90, 102, 105, 109, 153, 154, 155, 157
South Africa 9, 10, 32, 33, 75, 82, 101, 121, 155
space 50, 74, 163
safe space 147-148
status 51, 104, 146, 147
stepmother 34, 109, 120
Stones, Rosemary 67
StoryRide Project 134
storytelling 31, 33, 39, 40, 41, 73, 146, 154, 155
subtitling 94
symbol 12, 40, 50, 68, 96, 97, 98 see also Chapter 2
symbolising 20, 34, 50-51, 86, 89

Taishanese 121
tales
English 105
Tamarind Books 67
Tan, Shaun 20, 24, 45, 156
teachers 4, 6, 8, 13, 18, 30, 48-50, 60-62, 66-67, 83-85, 87, 91, 103, 112, 115, 122, 144-146, 149, 158, 163

technologies 7, 82-83,
television 9, 23, 39, 52, 64, 81-83, 88, 99
theatre 25, 41, 71, 80-82, 84, 142-144, 148, 165, 169
themes explored 38, 52, 68, 70, 78, 105
theory of mind 128
tones of voice, 144, 146
topsy-turvy world 144
Toy Story 12
traditional tales 67, 105, 117, 143
translation 93-108
Trevarthen, Colwyn 8
trickster tales 35, 154, 155

vocabulary 19, 125, 127, 130
voice 8, 15, 16, 22, 33, 40, 52, 53, 97, 99, 100, 115, 120, 121, 127, 129, 130, 132, 144, 146, 154, 157, 165, 167
authenticity 121-122
Vygotsky, Lev 10, 50, 95, 136, 142

Waddell, Martin 8, 68, 163
Wall*E 48
watching 23, 31, 45, 61, 54, 83, 88, 127
ways of doing 11, 31, 41, 59, 65, 67, 86, 90, 105, 115, 116, 126
Wilkins, Verna 67
Williams, A 145
Williams, Raymond 122
Wollman-Bonilla, J 84-5
written sound effects 23-24

The Year of the Flood 8
Yiddish 29-33